The Reader as
DETECTIVE

L E V E L C
Second Edition

Burton Goodman
*Former Teacher of English and Coordinator of High
School–College Continuum, Bureau of Educational
and Vocational Guidance, New York City Public Schools*

When ordering this book, please specify:
either **R 609 S** or READER AS DETECTIVE–C

Dedicated to serving

AMSCO

our nation's youth

AMSCO SCHOOL PUBLICATIONS, INC.
315 Hudson Street / New York, N.Y. 10013

Illustrations by John Jones

ISBN 1-56765-019-8

New York City Item 56765-019-7

Printed in the United States of America

1 2 3 4 5 6 7 8 9 10   00 99 98 97 96 95 94

TO THE STUDENT

The Reader as Detective has been specially designed to make you a more active reader—to help you become more involved in the reading process.

Today, more than ever, this is important because TV and movies can affect our reading habits. They, and other mass media, sometimes tend to make us passive, less active readers. This is unfortunate because reading is an active, participatory experience. It is not merely viewing or watching.

We believe that a good reader is an *active* reader, and that a good reader is like a good detective.

Think about this. When you read a powerful story of detection, suspense, mystery, or action, you march along with the characters in search of the ending, or solution. You *are*—or *should* become—THE READER AS DETECTIVE. Reading is an adventure—one in which you have become *involved*. Furthermore, the greater your involvement, the better reader you will become—and the more you will enjoy and appreciate reading.

This book will help make *you* THE READER AS DETECTIVE. It does this in a number of ways.

As noted above, the good reader must "march along with the characters in search of the ending, or solution." To encourage you to do this, each story in this volume contains a special and unique feature. It is called "Now it's time for YOU to be The Reader as Detective." This feature appears near the conclusion of each story. It provides you with an opportunity to be a reading detective—to guess how the story will end. After a while, you will learn to look for and discover clues and hints which will help you in this task.

A good reader is like a good detective in another way. To succeed, the detective must be able to gain an overall impression of the case, to recognize clues, identify important details, put events in sequence, draw inferences, and distinguish fact from opinion. Similarly, the effective reader must be a *reading* detective—on the search for the main idea, for supporting details, clues, inferences, and so forth. In a word, the reader, like the detective, must *master the skills* necessary to obtain successful results.

This volume provides ample opportunities for you to master these skills. Following each story are 25 short-answer questions. Questions 1 to 10 (**The Reader as Detective**) offer repeated practice in *the six basic reading skills* essential for achieving reading success. A symbol next to each question identifies the *kind* of reading skill that particular question helps you to develop. Each symbol is related to detection. Here are the symbols and the skills they represent:

THE SHERLOCK HOLMES HAT
  finding the *main idea*

A MAGNIFYING GLASS
  identifying *supporting details*

FINGERPRINTS
  finding *vocabulary clues*

A TRAIL OF FOOTPRINTS
  putting events in *sequence*

ILLUMINATED LIGHTBULB
  drawing *inferences*

SHERLOCK HOLMES PIPE
  distinguishing *fact from opinion*

Questions 11 to 15 (**Looking at Language**) help you understand elements of language such as descriptive language (powerful adjectives and vivid verbs), onomatopoeia, alliteration, similes, metaphors, synonyms, antonyms, homophones, compound words, and words in context.

Questions 16 to 25 (**Finding Word Meanings**) help you become a kind of word detective. By using context clue, and Cloze (sentence completion and sentence context) techniques, you will learn to develop vocabulary and reading skills.

A final section (**Thinking About the Case**) will help you sharpen your critical thinking skills.

The current edition contains a number of additional features including new and revised exercises, a Glossary, and easy identification of vocabulary words. To emphasize total communication skills (reading, writing, speaking, and listening), each **Thinking About the Case** section has been expanded.

The first story, "The Adventure of the Blue Diamond," introduces the master detective, Sherlock Holmes. To help familiarize you with the format of this volume, the story has been divided into three parts. In each part, you will note the *techniques*, or skills, that Holmes uses to solve the case. You will be encouraged to use similar techniques as you read.

There are 18 stories in this volume, one for every week of the term—or every *other* week of the school year. The stories, and the exercises which follow them, are intended to help you develop an *active, participatory* approach to reading. We are convinced that they can help you develop a very special kind of reading habit—one which will serve you for a lifetime. Now let's begin. It's time for *you* to become THE READER AS DETECTIVE.

Burton Goodman

ACKNOWLEDGMENTS

Grateful acknowledgment is made to the following sources for permission to reprint copyrighted stories. Adaptations are by Burton Goodman.

"Welcome to Our Bank," page 38. Reprinted by permission of Henry Slesar and his agents, Raines & Raines, 71 Park Avenue, New York. Copyright © 1960 by H.S.D. Publications, Inc.

"The Mother Goose Madman," page 49. By Betty Ren Wright. Copyright © 1959 by H.S.D. Publications, Inc. Reprinted by permission of Larry Sternig Literary Agency.

"The Love-Philtre of Ikey Schoenstein," page 62. From THE FOUR MILLION by O. Henry. Reprinted by permission of Doubleday & Company, Inc.

"Lucky Seven," page 71. Reprinted by permission of the author, Isaac Asimov.

"The Force of Luck," page 81. From CUENTOS: TALES FROM THE HISPANIC SOUTHWEST by Rudolpho A. Anaya and José Griego y Maestas. Reprinted by permission of Museum of New Mexico Press.

"A Trick of the Trade," page 95. Reprinted with permission from *Yankee* Magazine, published by Yankee Publishing, Inc., Dublin, N.H. 03444.

"Thank you, M'am," page 105. Reprinted by permission of Harold Ober Associates Incorporated. Copyright © 1958 by Langston Hughes. Copyright renewed 1986 by George Houston Bass.

"You Can't Take It With You," page 114. From ESCAPE IF YOU CAN by Eva-Lis Wuorio. Copyright © 1977 by Eva-Lis Wuorio. Reprinted by permission of Viking Penguin, Inc.

"Five Thousand Dollars Reward," page 134. Adapted from The Saturday Evening Post. Copyright © 1919 The Curtis Publishing Co.

"Shoes for Hector," page 144. From EL BRONX REMEMBERED

by Nicholasa Mohr. Copyright © 1975 by Nicholasa Mohr. Reprinted by permission of Harper & Row, Publishers, Inc.

"A Man Who Had No Eyes," page 154. Reprinted by permission of Layne Kantor Shroder and Tim Kantor.

"The Problem Solver and the Spy," page 163. Reprinted by permission of the author and the author's agents, Scott Meredith Literary Agency, Inc., 845 Third Avenue, New York, N.Y. 10022.

"The Turn of the Tide," page 175. Copyright © 1934 by C. S. Forester. Reprinted by permission of Harold Matson Company, Inc.

"Who's Cribbing?" page 189. Copyright © 1953 by Better Publications Inc. Reprinted by permission of agent Forrest J. Ackerman, 2495 Glendower Ave., Hollywood, CA 90027.

CONTENTS

The Adventure of the Blue Diamond

PART 1

by Arthur Conan Doyle

I had called upon my good friend, Mr. Sherlock Holmes, two days after Christmas, with the intention of wishing him the compliments of the season. He was sitting on the sofa, a pile of crumpled newspapers near at hand. Next to the sofa was a wooden chair, and on its back hung a very shabby round, felt hat, much the worse for wear, and cracked in several places. A magnifying glass on the seat of the chair suggested that the hat had been suspended there for the purpose of examination.

"You are busy," said I. "Perhaps I interrupt you."

"Not at all, Watson," said Holmes. "I am glad to have a friend with whom I can discuss the results of my investigation."

He pointed a finger in the direction of the old hat. "The matter is a perfectly trivial one, but there are some points in connection with it which are not entirely devoid of interest."

I seated myself in the armchair and warmed myself before the crackling fireplace, for a sharp frost had set in and the windows were covered with crystals of ice. "I suppose," I remarked, "that this hat, homely as it looks, has some deadly

1

story linked to it—that it is the clue which will guide you to the solution of some mystery and the punishment of some horrible crime."

"No, no. No crime," said Sherlock Holmes, laughing. "Just one of those odd little incidents which will occur when you have four million human beings all jostling each other within the space of a few square miles. Amid so dense a swarm of humanity, every possible combination of events may be expected to take place. Some, my dear Dr. Watson, may be unusual and bizarre without being criminal."

Holmes rose from the sofa and approached the chair. "Do you know Peterson, the transit inspector?"

"Yes."

"It is to him that this article belongs."

"It is his hat?"

"No, no; he found it. Its owner is unknown. However, Watson, I beg that you look upon this hat not as a battered bowler, but rather as a fascinating problem. But first, as to how it came here. It arrived Christmas morning along with a good fat goose. The facts are these. Early on Christmas morning, Peterson was walking on Tottenham Court. Peterson noticed a tall man walking with a slight limp. He was carrying a white goose slung over his shoulder.

"As the man reached the corner of Goodge Street, a fight suddenly broke out between this stranger and a gang of youths. One of the latter knocked off the man's hat. The man raised his cane to defend himself and, accidentally, smashed the shop window behind him. Peterson rushed forward to defend the stranger from his attackers. But the man, shocked at having broken the window, and seeing a person in uniform rushing toward him, dropped his goose, took to his heels, and vanished into the maze of small streets which lies behind Tottenham Court. The youths had also fled at the appearance of Peterson, so that he was left alone on the field of battle and in possession of this battered hat and a Christmas goose."

"Which surely he returned to their owner?"

"My dear Doctor Watson, there lies the problem. It is true that 'For Mrs. Henry Baker' was printed upon a small card which was tied to the bird's left leg. It is also true that the initials 'H.B.' are legible upon the lining of this hat. But as there are thousands of Bakers, and some hundreds of Henry Bakers in the city of London, it is not easy to restore lost property to any one of them.''

"What, then, did Peterson do?''

"He brought both the hat and the goose to me on Christmas morning, knowing that even the smallest problems are of interest to me. The goose we retained until this morning, when there were signs that, in spite of the cold weather, it would be advisable for it to be eaten without unnecessary delay. Peterson has carried it off, therefore, to fulfill the ultimate destiny of a goose, while I continue to retain the hat of the unknown gentleman who lost his Christmas dinner.''

"Did he not place an advertisement in the papers?''

"No.''

"Then what clue could you have as to his identity?''

"Only as much as we can deduce.''

"From his hat.''

"Precisely.''

"But you are joking. What can you gather from this old battered hat?''

"Here is my magnifying glass. You know my methods. What can you gather about the personality of the man who has worn this article?''

I took the tattered object in my hands, and turned it over rather ruefully. It was a very ordinary black hat of the usual round shape, hard, and much the worse for wear. The lining had been of red silk, but was very discolored. There was no maker's name, but, as Holmes had remarked, the initials "H.B." were scrawled upon one side. The elastic on the inside was missing. The hat was cracked, exceedingly dusty, and stained and spotted in several places, although there seemed to have been some attempt to hide the discolored patches by smearing them with ink.

"I can see nothing," said I, handing the hat back to my friend.

"On the contrary, Watson, you can see *everything*. You fail, however, to reason from what you see. You are too timid in drawing your inferences.''

"Then, please tell me what it is that you can infer from this hat.''

> Now observe the methods of Sherlock Holmes.
> They will be useful to *you* as The Reader as Detective.

Holmes picked up the hat and gazed at it in the very thoughtful fashion which was characteristic of him. "This hat suggests less than it might have," he remarked, "and yet there are a few inferences which are very distinct, and a few which are highly probable. That the man was highly intelligent is of course obvious. Also that he was fairly well-to-do three years ago, although he has now fallen upon difficult days and has seen the decline of his fortunes. It is clear, too, that his wife has ceased to pay much attention to him."

"My dear Holmes!"

"He has, however, retained some degree of self-respect," continued Holmes, disregarding my protest. "He is a man who does not lead an active life, goes out seldom, and is out of condition. He has gray hair which he has had cut within the last few days, and upon which he uses a lime hair cream."

"You are certainly joking, Holmes."

"Not in the least. But is it possible that even now when I give you these results, you are unable to see how they are attained?"

By way of answering, Holmes placed the hat upon his head. It came down over the forehead and settled upon the bridge of his nose. "It is simply a question of cubic capacity," said he. "A man with so large a brain must have something in it."

"But how did you know that he had fallen upon difficult days?"

"This hat is three years old. This style with the flat brim curled at the edges came in then. It is a hat of the very best quality. Look at the band of silk and the excellent lining. If this man could afford to buy so expensive a hat three years ago, and has bought no hat since, then he has certainly gone down in the world."

"Ah well, that is clear enough."

"Notice that he has endeavored to conceal some of these stains upon the felt by covering them with ink. This is a sign that he has not entirely lost his self-respect."

"Your reasoning is certainly plausible."

"The other points, that his hair is gray, that it has been recently cut, and that he uses lime hair cream are all to be gathered from a close inspection of the lower part of the lining. The magnifying glass discloses a large number of hair ends—clean cut by the scissors of the barber. They all appear to be sticking together, and there is the distinct odor of lime hair cream. Notice, too, this dust on the hat. It is not the gritty gray dust of the street, but the fluffy brown dust of the house, showing that it has been hanging up indoors most of the time. Furthermore, the marks of moisture upon the inside are proof that the wearer perspired very freely, and could, therefore, hardly be in the best of condition."

"But his wife—you said that she had ceased to pay him much attention."

"This hat has not been brushed for weeks. When I see you, my dear Watson, with many weeks' accumulation of dust upon your hat, and when your wife allows you to go out in such a state without pointing this out, I shall fear that she has ceased to pay you much attention."

"But he might be a bachelor."

"No, he was bringing home the goose to his wife. Remember the card upon the bird's leg."

"That is all very ingenious," said I, laughing, "but, since, as you said just now, there has been no crime committed, and no harm done except the loss of a goose, all this seems to be rather a waste of energy."

Sherlock Holmes had opened his mouth to reply, when the door suddenly flew open, and Peterson, the transit inspector, rushed into the room. He had flushed cheeks and the face of a man who is dazed with astonishment.

"The goose, Mr. Holmes! The goose, sir!" he gasped.

"Eh? What of it, then? Has it returned to life, and flapped off through the kitchen window?" Holmes twisted around on the sofa to get a better view of the man's excited face.

"See here, sir! See what my wife found in the goose!" He held out his hand, and displayed upon the center of his palm a brilliant, sparkling blue stone. It twinkled like a star in the hollow of his hand. We stared at its purity and radiance.

Sherlock Holmes whistled softly and sat up.

"Well, Peterson," said he, "this is a treasure indeed. I suppose you know what you've got in your hand."

"A diamond, sir! A precious stone! It cuts through glass as though it were putty."

"It's more than a precious stone. It's *the* precious stone."

"Not the Countess of Morcar's blue diamond!" I exclaimed.

"The very same. I ought to know its size and shape, seeing that I have been reading about it in *The Times* every day lately. It is absolutely unique and its value so great, it can only be guessed at."

Peterson plumped down into a chair, and stared from one to the other of us.

"It was stolen, if I remember correctly, at the Hotel Cosmopolitan," I remarked.

"Precisely so, on the twenty-second of December, just five

days ago. John Horner, a carpenter, was accused of having taken it from the lady's jewel case. The evidence against him was so strong that the case has been referred to the courts. I have some account of the matter here, I believe." Holmes rummaged amid his newspapers, glancing over the dates, until at last he smoothed one out, doubled it over, and read the following paragraphs:

"Hotel Cosmopolitan Jewel Robbery. John Horner, 26, a carpenter, was brought up on the charge of having, on the 22nd of December, extracted from the jewel case of the Countess of Morcar, the valuable gem known as the blue diamond.

"James Ryder, the chief attendant at the hotel, gave evidence to the effect that he had shown Horner up to the dressing room on the day of the robbery, in order to repair a broken shelf. He had remained with Horner for some time, but had finally been called away. On returning, he found that Horner had disappeared, that the bureau had been forced open, and that the small case in which the Countess kept the jewel was lying empty upon the dressing table. Ryder instantly called the police and Horner was arrested the same evening. The stone, however, could not be found upon his person or in his rooms.

"Catherine Cusak, maid to the Countess, reported hearing Ryder's cry of dismay on discovering the robbery, and to having rushed into the room, where she found matters as described by Ryder. Inspector Bradford gave evidence as to the arrest of Horner, who struggled frantically, and proclaimed his innocence in the strongest terms. Evidence of a previous conviction for robbery having been given against the prisoner, the magistrate referred the case for hearing. Horner, who had shown signs of intense emotion during the proceedings, fainted at the conclusion, and was carried out of the court."

"Hmm," said Holmes, thoughtfully, tossing aside the paper. "The question for us now to solve is the sequence of events leading from a stolen jewel at one side, to a goose in

Tottenham Court at the other. You see, Watson, our little deductions have suddenly assumed a much more important and less innocent aspect. Here is the diamond. The diamond came from the goose, and the goose came from Mr. Henry Baker, the gentleman with the bad hat. So now we must set ourselves very seriously to finding this gentleman, and discovering what part he has played in this little mystery."

> Now it's time for *YOU* to be a reading detective. The following exercises will help you accomplish this. Like Sherlock Holmes, you will learn to look for clues, find details, put events in sequence, and so forth. You will also learn to *anticipate*, or think ahead.
>
> Later, you will have an opportunity to solve THE ADVENTURE OF THE BLUE DIAMOND.

I. The Reader as Detective

Read each question below. Then write the letter of the correct answer to each question. Remember, the symbol next to each question identifies the *kind* of reading skill that particular question helps you to develop. Each symbol is related to detection.

Let's review the symbols.

 . . . finding the *main idea*

 . . . identifying *supporting details*

 . . . finding *vocabulary clues*

 . . . putting events in *sequence*

. . . drawing *inferences*

. . . distinguishing *fact from opinion*

1. Sherlock Holmes examined a hat which was

    a. worn and stained.   *c.* light gray in color.
    b. new and clean.

2. Who was accused of stealing the diamond?

    a. Mr. Peterson   *c.* Catherine Cusak
    b. John Horner

3. The initials "H.B." were "scrawled" upon one side of the hat. Which expression best defines the word *scrawled?*

    a. written hastily   *c.* lost or missing
    b. broken or crushed

4. Which happened last?

    a. Mr. Peterson brought Sherlock Holmes a Christmas goose.
    b. Holmes read aloud an account of a jewel robbery at the Hotel Cosmopolitan.
    c. Peterson's wife discovered the blue diamond.

5. We may infer that Sherlock Holmes will

    a. refuse to return the diamond to the Countess of Morcar.
    b. get into a fight with Inspector Bradford.
    c. look for the person who stole the diamond.

6. We learn that "the magistrate referred the case for hearing." What is the meaning of the word *magistrate?*

    a. victim   *c.* writer
    b. judge

7. According to Sherlock Holmes, the man who owned the hat

    a. was not married.
    b. was not very intelligent.
    c. had recently fallen on bad times.

8. Which of the following statements expresses an opinion?

   a. James Ryder called the police to report that the diamond was missing.
   b. Peterson attempted to help a man who had been attacked.
   c. Dr. Watson will probably be a great help to Sherlock Holmes in solving the mystery.

9. Clues in this selection suggest that the story takes place in

   a. London.
   b. New York City.
   c. a town in Scotland.

10. This chapter is mainly about

   a. how Dr. Watson met Sherlock Holmes.
   b. how a stranger got into a fight.
   c. a lost hat and a found diamond.

II. Looking at Language

Powerful adjectives and vivid verbs help to create **descriptive language.** As you know, an **adjective** is a word that describes a noun. Some examples of adjectives are *raging* river, *fierce* loyalty, *gigantic* error, and *dazed* boxer. Notice how these powerful adjectives help to create a picture, or produce an effect.

Answer the following questions about adjectives. Each one refers to "The Adventure of the Blue Diamond." Now you're looking at language!

11. "Sherlock Holmes was sitting on a sofa near a pile of crumpled newspapers." Which word in this sentence is an adjective?

   a. sitting
   b. crumpled
   c. newspapers

For practice, write an adjective of your own to replace the one in the sentence. (Note: one possibility is *crushed*. Think of another.)

12. Identify the powerful adjectives in the following sentence from the story: "I seated myself in the armchair and warmed myself before the crackling fireplace, for a sharp frost had set in."

a. seated, warmed
b. crackling, sharp
c. fireplace, frost

For practice, write two adjectives to replace the ones in the sentence.

13. Which one of the following sentences from the story contains an adjective?

a. What can you gather from this battered hat?
b. This hat has not been brushed for weeks.
c. One of the youths knocked off the hat.

14. Following are three expressions found in "The Adventure of the Blue Diamond." Which expression contains an adjective?

a. whistled softly
b. tattered object
c. gave evidence

For practice, replace the adjective in the expression with one of your own.

15. Below are three sets of words from the story. Which group contains powerful adjectives?

a. evidence, clue, property
b. took, whistled, struggled
c. fluffy, brilliant, sparkling

III. Finding Word Meanings

Now it's time to be a word detective. Following are ten words which appear in Part 1 of "The Adventure of the Blue Diamond." Study the words and the definitions beside them. Then complete the following sentences by using each vocabulary word only *once*. The first two words have already been added. They will help you get started. Now you're on your own!

NOTE: Do not write your answers in this book. Use a separate sheet of paper.

		page
trivial	not important	1
jostling	pushing; shoving	2
destiny	what finally becomes of a person or thing; one's fate	3
ruefully	in a bitter or sorrowful way	3
disregarding	ignoring; paying no attention to	4
plausible	reasonable; likely	5
ingenious	brilliant; unusually clever	5
precisely	exactly	6
extracted	drew out	7
aspect	a particular part of	8

16. Be certain to arrive at the theater early, for the curtain will go up <u>precisely</u> at eight o'clock.

17. "I wish I had never agreed to go skiing," Jason said <u>ruefully</u>, as he thought about his broken leg.

18. Since the difference in price is so slight, or _____ , let's pay the few extra pennies and buy the longer-life batteries.

19. At the back of the crowded subway car, people were _____ and pushing each other to get to the door.

20. Marge thought of a very original and creative solution to the problem; her brilliant idea was _____ .

21. The judge said, "Although your story is possible and might have taken place it is not very _____ ."

22. A person who keeps ignoring, or _____ , traffic signs is bound to get into an accident.

23. Which feature, or _____ , of the character's personality interested you the most?

24. It was Thomas Edison's _____ to eventually invent the electric light.

25. After a short pause, he slowly _____ his wallet from his pocket, and paid the bill.

IV. Thinking About the Case

Now it's time to think about the case. The questions in this section will help you sharpen your ability to think critically.

A. Sherlock Holmes is probably the most famous detective in literature. One reason for Holmes' popularity is his remarkable ability to discover clues and to use them to draw conclusions. Think about the story. Then show how Holmes drew conclusions from the clues he found.

B. Why do you think Arthur Conan Doyle, the creator of Sherlock Holmes, made Dr. Watson a character who is not especially skillful at detective work?

C. Over the years, numerous movies and television plays have been based on the adventures of Sherlock Holmes. Judging by what you have read so far, why do the tales of Sherlock Holmes lend themselves so well to dramatic presentation?

The Adventure of the Blue Diamond

PART 2

Dr. Watson looked closely at Sherlock Holmes. "But how," asked Watson, "shall we find this mysterious Mr. Baker?"

"To do this, we must try the simplest means first. And this lies, undoubtedly, in placing an advertisement in all the evening papers. If this fails, I have other methods."

"What will you say?"

"Give me a pencil and that slip of paper. Now then: 'Found at the corner of Goodge Street, a goose and a black felt hat. Mr. Henry Baker can have both by applying at 6:30 this evening at 221B Baker Street.' That is clear and concise."

"Very. But will he see it?"

"Well, he is sure to keep an eye on the papers, since, to a poor man, the loss was a heavy one. He was clearly so scared by his misfortune in breaking the window, and by the approach of Peterson, that he could think of nothing but fleeing. Since then he must have bitterly regretted the impulse which caused him to drop the goose. Then again, the mention of his name in the newspapers will cause him to see it, for everyone who knows him will point it out to him. Here you are, Peterson, run down to the advertising agency, and have this put in all the evening papers."

"Very well, sir. And this stone?"

"Ah, yes, I shall keep the diamond for the moment. Thank you. And I say, Peterson, just buy a goose on the way back, and leave it here with me, for we must have one to give this gentleman in place of the one which your family is now devouring."

When the transit inspector had left, Holmes took up the stone and held it against the light. "It's a pretty thing," said he. "Just see how it glints and sparkles. Of course it attracts crime. Every good stone does. It was found not twenty years ago on the bank of a river in China and it already has a sinister history. There have been two murders, an acid-throwing incident, a suicide, and several robberies brought about for the sake of this gem. I'll lock it up in my strongbox now, and drop a line to the Countess to say that we have it."

"Do you think that this man Horner is innocent?"

"I cannot tell."

"Well, then, do you imagine that this Henry Baker had anything to do with the matter?"

"It is, I think, much more likely that Henry Baker is an absolutely innocent man who had no idea that the bird which he was carrying had such considerable value. That, however, I shall determine if we have an answer to our advertisement."

"And you can do nothing until then?"

"Nothing."

"In that case, I shall return to my office. But I shall come back in the evening at the hour you mentioned, for I should like to see the solution of so tangled a business."

"I shall be very glad to see you then."

I had been delayed with a patient, and it was a little after half-past six when I found myself in Baker Street once more. As I approached the house, I saw a tall man with a coat which was buttoned to the chin, waiting outside. Just as I arrived, the door was opened, and we were shown up together to Holmes' rooms.

"Mr. Henry Baker, I believe," said Holmes, rising from his chair and greeting his visitor with a genial air which he could so readily assume. "This is my friend, Dr. Watson. Please take this seat by the fire, Mr. Baker. It is a cold night and you will be more comfortable there. Now then, is that your hat, Mr. Baker?"

"Yes, sir, that is undoubtedly my hat."

He was a large man, with rounded shoulders, a massive head, and a broad, intelligent face, sloping down to a pointed gray-brown beard. He spoke slowly, choosing his words with care, and giving the impression generally of a man of learning who had been ill-used at the hands of fortune.

"We have retained these things for some days," said Holmes, "because we expected to see an advertisement from you giving your address. I am at a loss now to know why you did not advertise."

Our visitor gave a rather shamefaced laugh. "Money is not so plentiful with me now, as it once was," he remarked. "I believed that the gang of roughs who assaulted me had carried off both my hat and the bird. I did not care to spend more money in a hopeless attempt at recovering them."

"Very naturally," said Holmes. "By the way, about the bird, we were compelled to eat it."

"To eat it!" Our visitor half rose from his chair in his excitement.

"Yes, it would have been no use to anyone had we not done so. But I presume that this other goose upon the sideboard, which is about the same weight and perfectly fresh, will answer your purpose equally well. After all, one bird is as good as another."

"Oh, certainly, certainly!" answered Mr. Baker with a sigh of relief.

"Well, then," said Sherlock Holmes, "there is your hat and there is your bird. By the way, would it bore you to tell me where you got the other one from? I am somewhat of a fowl fancier, and I have seldom seen a better-grown goose."

"Certainly, sir," said Baker. "A few of us often have lunch at the Alpha Inn near the British Museum. This year our good host, Windigate by name, started a goose club. Each member pays a small sum every week. In consideration for this, we each receive a bird at Christmas. My money having been duly paid, I was presented with a bird. You are familiar with the rest. I am indebted to you, Mr. Sherlock Holmes, for the return of my hat." Mr. Baker bowed solemnly to both of us, and strode off upon his way.

"So much for Mr. Henry Baker," said Holmes when he had closed the door behind him. "It is quite certain that he knows nothing whatever about the diamond. Are you hungry, Watson?"

"Not particularly."

"Then I suggest that we have a sandwich at the Alpha Inn to follow up on this clue while it is still hot."

"By all means, Holmes."

It was a bitter night, so we drew our coats warmly about us. Outside, the stars were shining coldly in a cloudless night, and the breath of passersby blew out smoke like so many pistol shots. In a quarter of an hour we were at the Alpha Inn. Once seated, we each ordered a sandwich from our white-aproned host.

"Your sandwiches should be excellent if they are as good as your geese," remarked Holmes.

"My geese?" The man seemed surprised.

"Yes, I was speaking only half an hour ago to Mr. Henry Baker, who was a member of your goose club."

"Ah, yes. But you see, sir, them's not *our* geese."

"Indeed. Whose are they, then?"

"Well, I got the two dozen for the club from a salesman in Covent Garden."

"Indeed! I know some of them well. Which one was it?"

"Breckenridge is his name."

"Ah well, I don't know him."

We finished our meal shortly. "Now, then, for Mr. Breckenridge," said Holmes, buttoning up his coat, as we came out into the frosty air. "Remember, Watson, that though we have so plain a thing as a goose at *one* end of this chain, we have at the *other* a man who will certainly receive seven years in prison unless we can establish his innocence. It is possible that our inquiry may confirm the guilt of Mr. John Horner. But, in any case, we have a line of investigation that has been missed by the police. Let us follow it to the bitter end."

We made our way to Covent Garden Market. One of the largest shops bore the name of Breckenridge upon it. The proprietor, a man with a sharp face and neat whiskers, was helping a boy to put up the shutters.

"Good evening. It's a cold night," said Holmes.

Breckenridge nodded, and shot a questioning glance at my companion.

"Sold out of geese, I see," continued Holmes, pointing at the bare slabs of marble.

"I can let you have five hundred tomorrow morning."

"That's no good."

"Well, there are some still left in the shop next door."

"Ah, but I was recommended to you."

"By who?"

"The landlord of the Alpha Inn."

"Oh, yes. I sold him a couple of dozen."

"Fine birds they were, too. Now where did you get them from?"

To my surprise, the question provoked a burst of anger from the shopkeeper.

"Now, then, mister," said he, "what are you driving at? Let's have it straight, now."

"It's straight enough," said Holmes. "I should like to know who sold you the geese which you sold to the Alpha."

"Well, then, I shan't tell you. So now!"

"Oh, it is a matter of very little importance. But I don't know why you should get so warm over a trifle."

"Warm! You'd be warm yourself if you were pestered as much as I am about those geese. '*Where are the geese?*' and '*Who did you sell the geese to?*' and '*Where are the geese now?*' One would think that they were the only geese in the world, to hear the fuss that's been made over them."

"Well, I have no connection with any other person or people who have been asking you questions about those geese," said Holmes, carelessly. "If you won't tell us, the bet I made is off, that's all. But I have a fiver on it that the bird I ate was bred in the country."

"Well, then, you've lost your fiver, for it was bred in the *town*," snapped the salesman.

"It's nothing of the kind."

"I say it is."

"I don't believe it."

"Do you think you know more about birds than I, I who have handled them ever since I was a boy? I tell you all those birds that went to the Alpha were bred in *town*."

"You'll never persuade me to believe that."

"Will you bet then?"

"It's merely taking your money, for I know that I am right.

But I'll place a sovereign* on it just to teach you not to be obstinate."

The salesman chuckled grimly. "Bring me the books, Bill," said he.

The small boy brought out a large volume and placed it beneath the hanging lamp.

"Now then, Mr. Know-it-all," said the salesman, "you see this book?"

"Well?"

"Here is the list of the folks from whom I buy. Do you see? Well then, here on these pages are the *country* folk, and the numbers after their names are where their accounts are in the book. Now then, you see these other pages in red ink. Well, that is a list of my *town* suppliers. Now look at the third name. Just read it out to me."

"Mrs. Oakshott, 117 Brixton Road," read Holmes. "Page 249."

"Quite so. Now turn to that page in the book."

Holmes turned to page 249. "Here you are. It says, 'Mrs. Oakshott, 117 Brixton Road. Egg and poultry supplier.'"

"Now then, what's the last entry? Never mind about the price."

"December 22. Twenty-four geese."

"Quite so. There you are. And underneath. What does it say?"

"Sold to Mr. Windigate of the Alpha Inn."

"What have you got to say now?"

Sherlock Holmes looked extremely unhappy. He drew a sovereign from his pocket and threw it down upon the table, turning away with the air of a man whose disgust is too deep for words. A few yards off, he stopped under a lamppost, and laughed in a hearty, noiseless fashion.

"I dare say," said Holmes, "that if I had put a hundred sovereigns down in front of that man he would not have given me such complete information as was drawn from him on the idea that he was beating me on a wager. Well, Watson, we are, I fancy, nearing the end of our quest. The only point to be determined is whether we should go on to this Mrs. Oakshott tonight, or whether we should wait until tomorrow. It

*sovereign: a British gold coin

is clear from what that fellow said that there are others besides ourselves who are interested in this matter. Therefore, we must—."

His remarks were suddenly cut short by a loud uproar which broke out from the shop which we had just left. Turning around, we saw a little rat-faced fellow standing in the center of the circle of yellow light which was thrown by the swinging lamp. Breckenridge, the salesman, framed in the door of his shop, was shaking his fists fiercely at the fearful figure.

"I've had enough of you and your geese!" Breckenridge shouted. "If you come pestering me anymore with your silly talk, I'll set the dog on you! What have you got to do with those geese? I bought them from Mrs. Oakshott. I didn't buy them from you!"

"No, but one of them was mine just the same," whined the little man.

"Well, then ask Mrs. Oakshott for it!"

"She told me to ask you."

"Well, you can ask the King of Prussia for all I care! I've had enough of this! Get out of here!" He rushed forward fiercely, and the little man darted off into the darkness.

> Now it's time for YOU to be The Reader as Detective.
>
> Who might this little man be? What connection might he have with the Countess' blue diamond?
>
> Try the following exercises. Then read the conclusion to "The Adventure of the Blue Diamond."

I. The Reader as Detective

Read each question below. Then write the letter of the correct answer to each question. Remember, the symbol next to each question identifies the *kind* of reading skill that particular question helps you to develop. Notice that each symbol is related to detection.

1. In order to find Henry Baker, Sherlock Holmes
   a. made an announcement on the radio.
   b. placed an advertisement in the newspapers.
   c. showed people pictures of him.

2. Henry Baker stated that he
   a. was very wealthy.
   b. did not own the hat which had been found.
   c. did not have a great deal of money.

3. The stone was found "on the bank of a river in China." As used in this sentence, what is the meaning of the word *bank*?
   a. place of business that handles money
   b. a sloping piece of land
   c. a row of elevators

4. Which happened last?
   a. Holmes and Watson went to the Alpha Inn.
   b. Holmes and Watson saw Mr. Breckenridge at Covent Garden.
   c. Holmes told Peterson that he would keep the stone.

5. Which one of the following statements expresses an opinion?
   a. Henry Baker was a large man with a gray-brown beard.
   b. Sherlock Holmes will probably be attacked by the little man.
   c. Mrs. Oakshott sold twenty-four geese to Mr. Breckenridge.

6. According to Holmes, the blue diamond
   a. had been found ten years earlier.
   b. was not really very valuable.
   c. had been the cause of several crimes.

7. We may infer that the man who was arguing with Mr. Breckenridge

    a. had nothing at all to do with the blue diamond.

    b. knew something about the blue diamond.

    c. had met Sherlock Holmes before.

8. Mr. Breckenridge loudly complained that he had often been "pestered" about the geese. Which expression best defines the word "pestered?"

    a. bothered or annoyed

    b. confused or bewildered

    c. cheated or overcharged

9. By losing a wager, Holmes learned that the geese came from

    a. the country.

    b. the town.

    c. a large city many miles away.

10. This chapter tells mainly about

    a. a meeting that Sherlock Holmes had with Henry Baker.

    b. how Holmes lost a wager to Mr. Breckenridge.

    c. how Holmes went about discovering where the diamond had come from.

II. Looking at Language

Like powerful adjectives, vivid verbs help to create **descriptive language.** As you know, a **verb** is a word that shows action. Some examples of verbs are *stumbled, sneered, gasped,* and *blinked.* Notice how these vivid verbs help to create a picture, or produce an effect.

Answer the following questions about verbs. Each question refers to the story.

11. "The salesman chuckled grimly." Identify the verb in this sentence from the story.

    a. salesman   *c.* grimly

    b. chuckled

For practice, write a verb of your own to replace the one in the sentence. (Note: one possibility is *laughed.* Think of another.)

12. Find the verbs in the following sentence from the story: ''He rushed forward fiercely, and the little man darted off into the darkness.''

   a. rushed, darted
   b. fiercely, darkness
   c. forward, little

For practice, write two verbs to replace the ones in the sentence.

13. Below are three sets of words found in this selection. Which group contains vivid verbs?

   a. robberies, investigation, advertisement
   b. bitter, innocent, hopeless
   c. attracts, assaulted, strode

14. Identify the vivid verb in the following sentence from the story: '''No, but one of them was mine all the same,' whined the little man.''

   a. mine
   b. whined
   c. little

For practice, replace the verb in the sentence with one of your own.

15. Following are three expressions found in Part 2 of ''The Adventure of the Blue Diamond.'' Which expression contains a vivid verb?

   a. the mysterious Mr. Baker
   b. in a cloudless night
   c. shot a questioning glance

III. Finding Word Meanings

Now it's time to be a word detective. Following are ten words which appear in Part 2 of ''The Adventure of the Blue Diamond.'' Study the words and their definitions. Then complete the following sentences by using each vocabulary word only *once*. The first word has already been added.

		page
concise	brief but full of meaning	14
sinister	evil; threatening	15
retained	kept; held	16
compelled	required; forced or commanded	16
duly	in a proper way or manner	16
indebted	obligated; owing	16
proprietor	owner	17
provoked	moved to action; bothered	18
obstinate	stubborn	20
quest	a search; hunt	20

16. Airline pilots are required, or <u>compelled</u>, to take frequent physical examinations.

17. When Jeff makes a decision, it's impossible to convince him to change his mind; he is very _____ .

18. Ponce de León looked all over the Florida peninsula in his ____ for the Fountain of Youth.

19. He usually plays the part of a villain because of his evil, or ____ look.

20. Her sharp and stinging remarks _____ the committee to take action.

21. The _____ paid us to clear the snow in front of the store.

22. I am very _____ to you for the wonderful letter of recommendation you wrote.

23. The play was about a man who lost his fortune, but _____ his honor.

24. The lawyer was very _____ ; she summed up her case with a few well-chosen words.

25. We will not be able to consider you for the job until your application is properly, or _____ completed.

IV. Thinking About the Case

A. What convinced Sherlock Holmes that Henry Baker knew "nothing whatever" about the diamond? How do you think Mr. Baker would have acted if he *had* known about the diamond?

B. Show how the scene between Sherlock Holmes and Mr. Breckenridge demonstrates that Holmes was quick-thinking and a good judge of character.

C. Arthur Conan Doyle, the creator of the Sherlock Holmes stories, was a master at producing vivid descriptions and sparkling dialogue. Find examples from the selection to support this statement.

"All the way there, every man I met seemed to be a policeman or a detective, and although it was a cold night, sweat was pouring down my face . . ."

The Adventure of the Blue Diamond

PART 3

Holmes and I stared at the retreating figure of the little man.

"Well," said Holmes, "this may save us a visit to Brixton Road. Come with me, and we will see what is to be made of this fellow." My companion quickly overtook the little man and touched him on the shoulder. He sprang around at once. "Who are you, then? What do you want?" he asked in a frightened voice.

"You will excuse me," said Holmes, "but I could not help overhearing your words with the salesman just now. I think that I could be of assistance to you."

"You? Who are you? How could you know anything of this matter?"

"My name is Sherlock Holmes. It is my business to know what other people don't know."

"But you can know nothing of this."

"Excuse me, I know everything of it. You are attempting to trace some geese which were sold by Mrs. Oakshott of Brixton Road to a salesman named Breckenridge, who in turn sold them to Mr. Windigate of the Alpha Inn, and by him to his club, of which Mr. Henry Baker is a member."

"Oh, sir, you are the very man I have longed to meet," cried the little man in a quivering voice. "I can hardly explain to you how interested I am in this matter."

Sherlock Holmes hailed a cab which was passing. "In that case, we had better discuss this in a cozy room rather than in this windy marketplace. But please tell me, before we go further, who it is that I have the pleasure of meeting."

The man hesitated for a moment. "My name is Frank Robinson," he said after a pause.

"No, no, your *real* name," said Holmes sweetly. "It is always awkward doing business with an alias."

The stranger flushed for a moment before answering. "Well, then," said he, "my real name is James Ryder."

"Precisely so. And you are the chief attendant at the Hotel Cosmopolitan. Please step into the cab, and I shall soon be able to tell you everything which you wish to know."

The little man stood glancing back and forth at Holmes and me. His eyes were half-hopeful and half-frightened, as one who is not sure whether he is on the verge of great luck or of catastrophe. Then he stepped into the cab and in half an hour we were back in his sitting room at Baker Street.

"Here we are," said Holmes cheerfully, as we marched into the room. "Please have a chair, Mr. Ryder. Now, then, you want to know what became of those geese?"

"Yes, sir."

"Or rather, I fancy, *that* goose. It was one bird, I imagine, in which you were interested—white, with a black mark across the tail."

Ryder was filled with emotion. "Oh," he cried, "can you tell me where it went to?"

"It came here."

"Here?"

"Yes, and a most remarkable bird it was. I'm not surprised that you should take such an interest in it. It laid an egg after it was dead—the brightest, most sparkling blue egg that ever was seen. I have it locked up here safely."

Our visitor staggered to his feet and grasped the edge of the table for support. Holmes unlocked his strongbox and held up the blue diamond which shone with a coldly brilliant radiance. Ryder stood glaring at the magnificent gem, uncertain whether to claim or disown it.

"The game's up, Ryder," said Holmes quietly. "Give it up, man, or you'll be in the fire. Help him back into his chair, Watson, for he looks quite pale."

For a moment, Ryder staggered. Then he sat staring at his accuser.

"I have," said Holmes, "almost every link in this case. But I need one or two points to make it complete. Now then, you had heard, Ryder, of this blue diamond of the Countess of Morcar's."

"It was Catherine Cusak who told me of it," he said in a cracking voice.

"I see. Her ladyship's waiting maid was your aide. Well, the temptation of sudden wealth so easily gained was too much for you. You knew that this man, John Horner, the carpenter, had been involved in a robbery before, and that suspicion would fall on him readily. What did you do, then? You arranged for some small job to be done in the Countess' room—you and your assistant Cusak—and you managed that he should be the man sent for. Then, when he had left, you broke into the jewel case, called the police, and had this unfortunate man arrested. You then—."

Ryder rose suddenly from the chair and clutched at Holmes' coat. "Please have mercy," he shrieked. "I never went wrong before! I never will again! Only don't bring this into court. Please don't!"

"Get back into your chair!" said Holmes sternly. "It is very well to cringe and crawl now, but you thought little enough of this poor Horner, in jail for a crime of which he knew nothing."

"I will flee, Mr. Holmes. I will leave the country. I will not appear as a witness against Horner. Then the charges against him will be dropped."

"Hmm, we will talk about that later. And now let us hear a true account of the next act. How the stone came into the goose, and how the goose came into the open market. Tell us the truth, for there lies your only hope of safety."

Ryder passed his tongue over his parched lips. "I will tell it just as it happened," he said. "After Horner was arrested, it seemed to me that it would be best for me to get away with the diamond at once, for I did not know at what moment the police might take it into their heads to search me and my room. There was no place about the hotel where it would be safe. I went out, as if on business, and I went to my sister's house. She had married a man named Oakshott and lived on

Brixton Road in town, where she bred geese for the market.

"All the way there, every man I met seemed to be a policeman or a detective, and although it was a cold night, sweat was pouring down my face before I came to Brixton Road. My sister asked me what the matter was, and why I was so pale, but I told her I was upset by the jewel robbery at the hotel. Then I went into the backyard and thought about what would be best to do.

"I had a friend named Maudsley who once served time in prison. One day we were talking about the ways of thieves and how they could get rid of what they stole. I knew that he

could help me out, so I made up my mind to go straight to Kilburn, where he lived, and take him into my confidence. He would show me how to turn the diamond into money. But how to get to him in safety. That was the problem. I thought of the thousand agonies I had gone through in coming from the hotel. I might at any moment be seized and searched, and there would be the stone in my pocket.

"I was leaning against the wall at the time, and looking at the geese which were waddling about at my feet. Suddenly an idea came into my head which showed me how I could evade the police and beat the best detective that ever lived.

> Now it's time for YOU to be The Reader as Detective.
>
> What was John Ryder's plan for getting rid of the diamond? What might have gone wrong?
>
> Think back to the events of the story. You should now be able to trace the path of the Countess' blue diamond.
>
> Read on to see if you are right!

"My sister had told me some weeks before that I might have the pick of her geese for a Christmas present, and I knew that she was always as good as her word. I would take my goose now, and in it I would carry my stone to Kilburn.

"I caught one of the birds, a fine big one, white, with a black mark across its tail. Opening its bill, I thrust the stone down into its throat as far as my fingers could reach. The bird gave a little gulp, then was perfectly content. At that moment, my sister came in. As I turned to speak to her, the bird broke loose, and fluttered off among the others.

"'Whatever were you doing with that bird, Jim?' says she.

"'Well,' said I, 'you said you'd give me one for Christmas, and I was just checking to see which one was the fattest.'

"'Oh,' says she, 'we've set yours aside already. Jim's bird, we call it. It's the big, white one over there. We have twenty-six birds, which makes one for you, and one for us, and two dozen to sell.'

"'Thank you, Maggie,' says I, 'but if it's all the same to you, I'd rather have that bird I was looking at.'

"'Well,' she says, 'the one we picked is a good three pounds heavier. We fattened it especially for you.'

"'Never mind. I prefer the other, and I'll take it now,' said I.

"'Oh, just as you like,' said she, a little annoyed. 'Which is the one you want, then?'

"'That white one with the black mark on its tail.'

"'Oh, very well. Take it, it's yours.'

"Well, that's what I did Mr. Holmes, and I carried that bird all the way to Kilburn. When I told my pal what I had done, he laughed until he choked, he thought it so hilarious. But later, when we made a meal of the bird, my heart turned to water. For there was no sign of the diamond, and I knew that some terrible mistake had been made. I rushed back to my sister's house, and hurried into the backyard. There was not a goose to be seen there.

"'Where are all the birds, Maggie?' I cried.

"'Gone to the dealer, Jim.'

"'Which dealer?'

"'Mr. Breckenridge in Covent Garden.'

"'But was there another goose?' I asked, 'a white one with a black mark across its tail, the same as the one I chose?'

"'Yes, Jim, there were two like that, and I could never tell them apart.'

"Well, then, of course I saw what had happened. I ran off as fast as my legs would carry me to this man Breckenridge. But he had sold the entire lot, and not one word would he tell me as to where they had gone. You heard him yourself to-night. I went back again and again, but he always refused to answer my questions. My sister thinks that I am going mad. Sometimes I think that I am myself. And now—and now I am myself a thief and a scoundrel, without ever having touched the wealth for which I sold my character. Help me! Help me!" He burst into sobs, with his face buried in his hands.

There was a long silence, broken only by his heavy breathing, and by the measured tapping of Sherlock Holmes' finger tips upon the edge of the table. Then my friend rose and threw open the door.

"Get out!" said he.

"What, sir? Oh, bless you!"

And no more words were needed. There was a clatter upon the stairs, the bang of a door, and the sound of footsteps running down the street.

"After all, Watson," said Holmes, "we shall notify the Countess that her diamond has been recovered. If Horner were in danger it would be another thing. But this fellow Ryder will not appear as a witness against him, and without his testimony the case will be dropped. I do not think that Ryder will go wrong again. He is too terribly frightened. Send him to jail now and you may make him a jailbird for life. Besides, Doctor, it is the season of forgiveness. Therefore, on this occasion, let us forgive and forget.''

I. The Reader as Detective

Read each question below. Then write the letter of the correct answer to each question. Remember, the symbol next to each question identifies the *kind* of reading skill that particular question helps you to develop.

1. At first, John Ryder told Sherlock Holmes that

   a. he was a friend of Henry Baker.
   b. he was not very interested in tracing the geese.
   c. his name was Frank Robinson.

2. When Ryder stole the diamond, he knew that suspicion would fall upon

   a. John Horner.   *c.* himself.
   b. Catherine Cusak.

3. The blue diamond shone ''with a coldly brilliant radiance.'' What is the meaning of the word *radiance*?

   a. great worth
   b. striking brightness
   c. dull surface

4. Which happened last?

   a. Holmes threw open the door and told Ryder to get out.
   b. Ryder returned to his sister's house and hurried into the backyard.
   c. Ryder rushed to Covent Garden and questioned Mr. Breckenridge.

5. We may infer that Ryder

   a. didn't care which bird he took from his sister's house.
   b. left his sister's house with the wrong bird.
   c. wanted the fattest bird that he could find.

6. Which one of the following statements does *not* express an opinion?

    a. Ryder will surely commit some other crimes.

    b. Breckenridge refused to answer Ryder's questions.

    c. Holmes probably made a mistake in letting Ryder go.

7. Ryder stated that he wished to visit a friend in Kilburn to "take him into my confidence." As used in this sentence, which expression best defines the word *confidence*?

    a. a strong belief in one's ability

    b. a trick or joke

    c. trust or secrecy

8. Holmes' action at the conclusion of the story suggests that he was

    a. very hard-hearted.

    b. a merciful person.

    c. not interested in saving John Horner.

9. What was true of the goose that Ryder selected?

    a. It was the smallest one that Mrs. Oakshott owned.

    b. It looked just like all the other geese.

    c. It was white with a black mark across its tail.

10. Part 3 of the story tells mainly about

    a. how Sherlock Holmes found James Ryder.

    b. Ryder's confession to Sherlock Holmes.

    c. a jewel robbery at the hotel.

II. Looking at Language

As you have learned, powerful adjectives and vivid verbs help to create descriptive language. The following questions, based on Part 3 of "The Adventure of the Blue Diamond," will help you review adjectives and verbs.

11. Holmes suggested to Ryder that they "discuss this in a cozy room." Which one of the following words is an adjective?

    a. discuss   *b.* cozy   *c.* room

12. Following are three expressions found in this selection. Identify the expression that contains an adjective.
   a. called the police
   b. stepped into the cab
   c. magnificent gem

   For practice, replace the adjective in the expression with one of your own.

13. "Our visitor staggered to his feet and grasped the table for support." Identify the verbs in this sentence.
   a. visitor, table
   b. feet, support
   c. staggered, grasped

   For practice, write two verbs to replace the ones in the sentence.

14. "Ryder rose suddenly from the chair and clutched pitifully at Holmes' coat." Which words from the sentence are verbs?
   a. rose, clutched
   b. suddenly, pitifully
   c. chair, coat

15. Following are three sets of words found in the story. Which group contains vivid verbs?
   a. shrieked, choked, sprang
   b. remarkable, windy, little
   c. companion, thieves, carpenter

III. Finding Word Meanings

Now it's time to be a word detective. Below are ten words which appear in Part 3 of "The Adventure of the Blue Diamond." Study the words and their definitions. Then complete the following sentences by using each vocabulary word only *once*.

16. The frightened dog put its tail between its legs and began to shiver and _____with fear in its eyes.

17. After spending many hours in the desert, the exhausted traveler was hot, weary, and _____ .

18. Do not try to dodge, or _____ , your responsibility.

19. After several months, the police finally caught the _____ who had been setting the fires.

20. The prisoner was convicted by the _____of a passerby who was a witness to the crime.

21. To avoid being recognized, the movie star wore a disguise and gave a(n) _____rather than her real name.

22. In 1871, a fire in Chicago killed hundreds of people; it was a terrible _____ .

23. Although the commissioner could not meet with our group, her _____was able to assist us.

24. The speech was so _____ , the audience could hardly stop laughing.

25. According to the report, scientists are very close to finding a cure for the disease; they are on the _____of success.

IV. Thinking About the Case

A. Suppose Sherlock Holmes had not become involved in this case. What do you think would have happened to John Horner? To Catherine Cusak? To the Countess' blue diamond?

B. Do you think James Ryder will ''go wrong'' again? Give reasons to support your answer.

C. Suppose that you were directing a television episode based on this selection. What suggestions would you give to the actor playing Sherlock Holmes? That is, which of Holmes' character traits do you think should be stressed?

Welcome to Our Bank

by Henry Slesar

"Star light, star bright, first star I see tonight, I wish I may, I wish I might, have the wish I wish to-night. Please let the First Central Bank be robbed."

George Picken said this rhyme softly to himself as he looked up at the bright star that appeared over the town of Southwick Corners. George had been repeating this childish verse for years, almost since the day he started to work at the bank six years ago, as an assistant teller. Now he was a regular teller, with a brass nameplate and a cash box all his own. Once he had thought that this was all he would ever desire in life. But soon he learned different. He found that it wasn't the job, or the title, that really mattered. It was the money—so crisp, so green, so crackling with promise, so unlike the meager pay check he received every other week. Sometimes, there was as much as *fifty thousand dollars* in his hands, fifty thousand green passports to the pleasures and comforts of the larger, brighter world beyond Southwick Corners.

George was a Bothwick Boy, and that meant he couldn't steal the money himself. Bothwick Boys, graduates of that long-honored school, were taught that stealing was wrong. No Bothwick Boy had ever been arrested for stealing. No Bothwick graduate *stole*.

And besides, there were three people whom George couldn't disappoint. One was Mr. Burrows, the bank president, who had given him the job. The second was Aunt Phyllis, who had raised George. The third was Jennifer, who would probably marry George once he named the day.

No, George Picken knew he could never simply *take* the thick wads of bills that were always under his hand. There was really only one solution. The First Central Bank must be *robbed*. He thought about it constantly, especially when he flipped open his morning paper and found items about bank holdups in all parts of the country. Everybody seemed to be robbing banks these days. Even little old ladies were shoving threatening notes through tellers' windows. There was hardly a bank in America that *hadn't* been robbed, thought George sourly. Except, of course, the First Central Bank of Southwick Corners. What was *wrong* with his bank? Did would-be bank robbers hold the bank's petty four million dollars in contempt? Were they frightened of Mr. Ackerman, the ancient bank guard who hadn't touched his gun holster in twenty-two years? Or was it just plain bad luck?

Mournfully, George Picken trudged home from his chores every day, and asked himself these questions. Why, why, why? With bank robberies on the increase, why couldn't *he* get robbed?

Naturally, there was a method to George's madness. It was a method which had occurred to him long, long before. The scheme was simple, and it went like this:

If Bank Robber A holds up Bank Teller B . . .

And if Teller B gives Bank Robber A a certain amount of money . . .

Who is to know *how much* money Bank Robber A received from Teller B?

What is to prevent Teller B from pocketing all the money left and claiming it was stolen by Bank Robber A?

It was simple, and every time George Picken thought about the plan, it seemed more certain.

There was only one flaw.

Where was Bank Robber A?

One morning, George Picken awoke with a strange sense that something would happen today. His Aunt Phyllis was aware that he was troubled the moment she saw him at the breakfast table.

"You sick, George?"

"No, Aunt Phyllis. Why do you say that?"

"You *look* sick. Must be those lunches you eat downtown. Maybe you better come home for lunch from now on. Some good home cooking will fix you up."

"I'm all right," George Picken said.

On his way to work, he met Jennifer, and had a sudden urge to tell her something.

"Jennifer—"

"Yes, George?"

"Jennifer, about that—matter we were talking about. You know."

She blushed. "Yes, George?"

"I just wanted you to know. It won't be long from now, Jennifer. I have a feeling about it."

George walked into the bank and headed for his teller's cage. Mr. Burrows, the president, greeted him with a nod.

"Morning, Mr. Burrows," he said cheerfully. "It's a *wonderful* day, isn't it?"

Mr. Burrows blinked in astonishment, grumbled, and went into his office.

At two o'clock, the bank door opened and Bank Robber A walked in.

There could be no doubt about the fact that he was a bank robber—not for a moment. For one thing, he *slinked* in. The everyday customer of the First Central usually strolled into the bank. They *never* slinked. Even more convincing was the fact that the man wore a white handkerchief over the lower part of his face. Nobody in Southwick Corners wore a mask, except at Halloween.

"All right," the man said in a deep voice. "This is a stickup."

He took an ugly revolver from his right-hand pocket. Mr.

Ackerman, the guard, made a low, squeaky sound. "You," the Bank Robber said to him. "Lie down on the floor." Mr. Ackerman sighed and lay down like an old obedient pet dog.

Mr. Burrows came out of his office. He grunted when he saw the bandit, and started back where he came from. The Bank Robber asked him, politely, to return. Mr. Burrows, grumbling in discontent, did as he was told. Then the man in the mask stepped up to George Picken's cage.

George sighed in relief. There were two tellers' cages, his own and Miss Tyler's, and it was a toss-up as to who would get the business. Luckily, the robber had chosen him.

"All right," the man said. "Hand it over."

"Yes, sir," George said brightly. "Any particular way you would like the bills?"

"Just hand it over!"

George reached into his cash box, and took all the bills from the top compartments. The total was close to six thousand dollars. There was another layer below, containing thousands more. He passed the bills through the window, and the Bank Robber took them greedily. Then he stuffed them into his pocket, and dashed back towards the exit.

Then, while all eyes watched the retreat of Bank Robber A, George calmly lifted off the top of the cash box, and quickly slipped the largest possible bills into his trouser pockets.

The door swung outwards, and the bank robber was gone.

"Call again on our bank," George thought.

Then he fainted.

When he stirred and awoke, his first concern was that he had been searched. He touched his trouser pockets and felt the bills there. He smiled up at the concerned faces that surrounded him.

"I'm all right," he said bravely. "I'm perfectly okay."

"Wasn't that awful?" Miss Tyler, the other teller said, her eyes bright with excitement. "Did you ever see anything so brazen in your life?"

"Never," George agreed. "Mr. Burrows—"

"Mr. Burrows went to call the police," Mr. Bell, the chief auditor said. "You sure you don't want a doctor, George?"

"No, no, I'm all right. If I could just go home now—"

"I think you should," Miss Tyler said. "I really think you should, Mr. Picken. What an awful experience."

"Yes," George said. "It was really awful."

A few minutes later, he was out on the street. He didn't count the money until he was safely behind his bedroom door. It was seven thousand five hundred dollars. He was very happy.

He slept late the next morning, feeling he owed it to himself. When he awoke, his Aunt Phyllis told him that someone from the bank had called, inquiring about his health. She had said that he was all right, but in need of rest, and would probably take the day off.

"Oh, no," he said firmly, for he must continue to appear a hardworking and loyal bank teller. "Can't do that, Aunt Phyllis. There's work to be done."

"Now, now," his aunt said. "Your health comes first. Besides, they're not opening the bank for business today. I think they're having a special audit or something."

"All the more reason for me to go," George said, as a Bothwick Boy would say.

He dressed and went downtown. As soon as he arrived, he saw that his aunt had been correct. The First Central Bank was definitely not open for business, even if all the employees were present. But the strangest impression he received upon entering was that the bank's personnel were exceptionally cheerful. Miss Tyler was smiling broadly. Mr. Bell, busy with his adding machine, winked at him. Old Mr. Ackerman was rocking on his heels, his hands locked behind his back, looking as calm and placid as ever. And when he was told to enter Mr. Burrow's office, he opened the door and found the bank president unusually friendly and genial.

"You wanted to see me, Mr. Burrows?"

"Oh, yes! Come in, George! I want you to meet somebody, George—an old friend of yours." Mr. Burrows chuckled with amusement.

Now George saw the man in the chair. He recognized him at once as Mr. Carruthers, the ex-president of the First Central Bank and the current Chairman of the Board of Directors. Mr. Carruthers, a fine, spruce gentleman in his late sixties, smiled quizzically and nodded his head in greeting.

"Good morning, George," he said. "Sorry to hear about your trouble yesterday. Are you all right now?"

"Oh, yes, sir, Mr. Carruthers, I'm just fine."

"Good, glad to hear it." He laughed lightly. "That was quite a little adventure, George, wasn't it? Just goes to show how easy it is to rob our little bank, doesn't it? We were pretty smug about it, weren't we?"

"Sir?"

Mr. Burrows chuckled again. "Don't let him tease you anymore, George. He's had enough fun for a while. Will you tell him, Dan, or should I?"

"Oh, I guess it's my duty."

Mr. Carruthers scratched his chin. "George, I was sorry to give you a hard time, but I thought it would be a good idea, considering all the banks being robbed these days, to prove that our bank can be robbed, too. That's why I played my little game yesterday, just to keep everybody on their toes. It might seem pretty silly, but I think we all learned something, don't you?"

George was confused. "I don't understand," he said. "What game? What do you mean?"

> Now it's time for YOU to be The Reader as Detective.
>
> What *did* Mr. Carruthers mean? What "game" was he talking about? Clues in the story will help you answer these questions.
>
> Read on to see if you are right!

Mr. Carruthers laughed, and pulled out a white handkerchief from his trouser pocket. He placed it over his mouth and said: "All right. Hand it over!"

Mr. Burrows laughed heartily, but George wasn't able to join in.

"And the money?" George said, in a choked voice.

"Oh, don't worry about that," Mr. Carruthers said. "I put it all back in your cash box, George. We're just finishing up the audit now." He got up and walked over to clap George on the shoulder. "You're a good lad, George, a good lad. Bothwick Boy, aren't you?"

"Yes, sir," said George Picken weakly.

Behind them, the door opened and Mr. Bell, the chief auditor, poked his head into the room. "Mr. Burrows," he said very seriously. "May I see you a moment?"

I. The Reader as Detective

Read each question below. Then write the letter of the correct answer to each question. Remember, the symbol next to each question identifies the *kind* of reading skill that particular question helps you to develop.

1. What mattered most to George about his job was
   a. the title.
   b. the responsibility.
   c. the money that went through his hands.

2. Mr. Burrows was

   a. a guard at the bank.

   b. the bank president.

   c. the Chairman of the Board of Directors.

3. When George "stirred and awoke, his first concern was that he had been searched." As used in this sentence, what is the meaning of the word *stirred?*

   a. mixed up

   b. put together

   c. moved about

4. What happened last?

   a. George told Jennifer that he thought they would be able to get married soon.

   b. Mr. Carruthers explained that he had played a little game.

   c. A bank robber told George to hand over the money.

5. At the end of the story, Mr. Bell, the chief auditor, asked Mr. Burrows, "May I see you a moment?" Probably, he is going to tell Mr. Burrows that

   a. all the money has been returned to the bank.

   b. the sum of seven thousand five hundred dollars is still missing from George's cash box.

   c. the audit revealed nothing unusual.

6. When George returned to the bank after the robbery, he was surprised to find that

   a. everyone seemed very cheerful.

   b. the robber had already been captured.

   c. Miss Tyler was suspicious of him.

7. Which one of the following statements expresses an opinion?

   a. The bank president will probably just warn George and let him keep his job.

   b. Six years ago, George began working at the bank as an assistant teller.

   c. George had been raised by his Aunt Phyllis.

8. Mr. Ackerman looked ''as calm and placid as ever.'' Which expression best defines the word *placid*?

    a. quiet or peaceful   *c.* tired or exhausted

    b. angry or upset

9. George thought he was lucky because

    a. there had never been a robbery at his bank.

    b. the bank robber chose his cage rather than Miss Tyler's.

    c. his job at the bank paid him very well.

10. This story tells mainly about

    a. a man's scheme for robbing a bank, and how the plan failed.

    b. how George needed some money to marry Jennifer.

    c. a loyal bank teller who loved his job.

II. Looking at Language

When a word *sounds* like the thing it *describes*, this is known as **onomatopoeia**. Some examples of onomatopoeia are *splash*, *hiss*, *crunch*, and *buzz*. Say these words softly to yourself. Notice how each *sounds* like the thing it describes. Like descriptive language, onomatopoeia helps to create a picture, or produce an effect.

Answer the following questions. Each one relates to onomatopoeia.

11. George thought that the money was ''so green, so crackling with promise.'' Select the word that illustrates onomatopoeia.

    a. green   *b.* crackling   *c.* promise

12. ''Mr. Ackerman, the guard, made a low, squeaky sound.'' Which word in this sentence sounds like the thing it is describing?

    a. guard   *b.* made   *c.* squeaky

13. Below are three sets of words from the story. Which group of words contains examples of onomatopoeia?

    a. grumbling, scratched, choked

    b. steal, learned, taught

    c. notes, lunch, game

14. Mr. Burrows "grunted when he saw the bandit, and started back where he came from." Which word in this sentence is an example of onomatopoeia?

   a. grunted   *b.* saw   *c.* bandit

15. Which sentence contains an example of onomatopoeia?

   a. Mr. Burrows came out of his office.
   b. Mr. Burrows chuckled with amusement.
   c. Mr. Burrows did as he was told.

III. Finding Word Meanings

Now it's time to be a word detective. Below are ten words which appear in "Welcome to Our Bank." Study the words and their definitions. Then complete the following sentences by using each vocabulary word only *once*.

		page
meager	thin or lean; slight	38
wads	small packs, usually of soft material	39
flaw	a slight error or mistake	40
discontent	unhappy; not satisfied	41
brazen	bold; having no shame	42
audit	an examination of records or accounts	42
exceptionally	unusually; to an extraordinary degree	43
genial	friendly; pleasant	43
quizzically	in a questioning way; puzzlingly	43
smug	too pleased with one's self	43

16. Once a year, the bank has a(n) _____of its records to make sure that all the accounts are correct.

17. The experiment worked perfectly; there was not the smallest oversight, error, or _____ .

18. The restaurant served such _____portions, we were still hungry after the meal.

19. If you pack the vase in _____of paper, I do not think it will be broken in delivery.

20. Manuela is a(n) _____fine writer; her short stories have won many awards.

21. The robberies were committed by a gang of reckless, or _____ , thieves who always worked in broad daylight.

22. His strange actions confused us all; we could do nothing but stare _____and wonder.

23. If you are _____with your current job, perhaps you should seek employment elsewhere.

24. Even though Gene loses whenever he plays tennis, he always remains cheerful and _____on the court.

25. We could tell instantly that Roberta knew the answer to the question because of the very self-satisfied, or _____ , look on her face.

IV. Thinking About the Case

A. At the end of the story, Mr. Carruthers tells George, "You're a good lad, George, a . . . . Bothwick Boy. . . ." Why was being a "Bothwick Boy" important to George? How did being a "Bothwick Boy" affect his actions?

B. Imagine that the story continues and that Mr. Burrows accuses George of stealing seven thousand five hundred dollars. What do you think George would say to Mr. Burrows?

C. When something occurs which is the opposite of what might naturally be expected, this is known as irony. What is ironic in "Welcome to Our Bank"?

The Mother Goose Madman

by Betty Ren Wright

Julia Martell looked closely at the envelope—the one that started the terror. Only one thing distinguished it from the twenty she had already opened. The other envelopes were addressed to Children's Books Editor, Webster Publishing Company. This one was addressed to Julia Martell, Editor of Children's Books.

Julia noticed the difference, but took no pleasure in it. She preferred to remain nameless, anonymous in her job. That was because it so often consisted of saying no to people, of rejecting manuscripts which had been submitted. As a rule, she barely glanced at the letters, but turned, at once, to the manuscripts themselves.

Julia opened the envelope and pulled out a single sheet of paper. *Dear Miss Muffet*, the letter began. Julia sighed at this cute approach. She continued reading. *Under separate cover please find my little contribution. It has been planned with you and no one else in mind. I hope it proves useful. If not, you will hear from me again. Sincerely, J. Smith.*

Now Julia was curious. She glanced over the packages, looking for one in the same handwriting. There it was, stamped FRAGILE and HANDLE WITH CARE in a half-dozen places.

49

Fred, his arms filled with art boards, stopped beside her desk.

"Must be worth its weight in gold," he said.

"Then it's not worth much," Julia said dryly. "It feels empty."

She slipped off the wrapping. The box was filled with long, thin strips of paper, as though to protect something delicate inside. Within the box, a feathery scrap of black showed through. Julia moved the pieces of paper aside.

Her first reaction was disbelief. But there it was: the spider's black hairy body drawn up over folded legs, the tremor of its body as the paper was shifted. Then the legs moved.

"Oh!" she exclaimed. "Oh, *no!*"

She recoiled because of her dread of all crawling things, while Fred slammed the heavy art boards down on the spider.

The brightly lit drugstore was not far from her home. Julia stopped there every evening on her way from the bus to pick up a paper. Often she would reorder the eyewash that made her hours of reading possible. Possibly she liked the store because it reminded her of the one in which she had worked during her college days. Certainly her feeling about the place had nothing to do with the clerks and pharmacist who went about their business with detached and monotonous regularity.

Now Julia waved her prescription at the white-coated man in the back of the store. She placed the slip on the counter, picked up a newspaper, and dropped some change beside the prescription.

"Anything else?" the man called to her.

"No," Julia said, but with some reluctance. The cheerful store was especially soothing after the unpleasantness of the afternoon.

Partly, of course, she was disturbed by the fuss that everyone had made. There was Fred, his eyes showing more concern than his comments. Then there were the copyreaders and the secretaries who had pondered about Miss Muffet and her spider until it was time to go home. Even Mr. Webster had come in, curious about the excitement in the usually subdued editorial offices.

Julia hated their attention. She always felt much more comfortable alone. But it was more than the attention of her fellow workers that had upset her. And it was more than the fact of the spider. She was disturbed because there was, somewhere, a person who called himself J. Smith, who, she felt, hated her with a very real hate. She, who had tried so hard to remain cool and aloof, was caught in the entanglement of another person's deep emotion.

Julia hurried down the block to her own apartment building. She opened the door of her mailbox and took out a handful of letters. Bills. Two invitations to book conferences. A letter from her aunt in Maine, writing to thank her for a birthday present.

And an envelope addressed to Julia Martell, Editor of Children's Books.

Julia put the other letters into her bag, opened the door of the elevator and stepped in. Almost eagerly, she opened the envelope. It was the same kind of paper, she saw that at once, the same slanted handwriting. But she also saw that the salutation was different.

Dear Miss Humpty Dumpty, Did you enjoy my first contribution? Expect another one soon.

The elevator lurched upward, slowed, halted. The doors opened and she faced her familiar hallway. She stepped out and waited for her heart to stop its violent thumping.

Humpty Dumpty had a great fall—

It wouldn't be, Julia thought, in the elevator, or here in the hallway, where one of the other tenants might be the victim. But it might be inside her apartment, or possibly . . .

Julia turned into the dark corridor that led to her door. If she had been moving along at her usual brisk pace, she would have had a very bad fall. But caution had slowed her steps. Therefore she stopped at once when the wire brushed her left ankle. It was a thin, gray wire—the same shade as the carpeting—stapled to the paneling on both sides of the corridor, about three inches above the floor. From three feet away, it could hardly be seen.

Julia stared hard. After a moment, she took a white linen handkerchief from her bag, and draped it over the wire as a warning to anyone else who might be coming along. Inside her apartment, she looked carefully in the bedroom, the kitchen, the bath. Then she came back into the living room and called the police.

The next morning, Julia took the manuscript rejection files into the small conference room and closed the door behind her. The police believed that her correspondent was a dissatisfied and disgruntled amateur writer, a fanatic, one whose manuscript had been rejected. If this were so, she would determine his identity herself. His handwriting was distinctive—slanting, with unfinished loops on the rising letters, a twisted cross on the *t*, and narrow *o*'s. She would recognize it!

In the rejection file, there was only one letter from a J.

Smith. It was written in a barely legible scrawl. Accompanying it was a story about the writer's childhood long ago. The letter was signed *Jack Smith, age eighty-nine*, and was two years old.

That couldn't be the one, thought Julia, and she patiently began to look through the file again. The lieutenant had warned her that J. Smith was probably a pseudonym, and common sense told her that the writer, even though he had taken no pains to disguise his handwriting, would hardly sign his name to what would be evidence against him.

She was halfway through the third drawer in the file, when the door opened and Fred came in.

"Any luck?" he asked.

She shook her head.

"Everybody's guessed," he said, "what you're doing in here. And at least six people volunteered to help your secretary sort your mail this morning . . . Didn't find a thing."

Julia frowned. "I wish they'd just forget it," she said. "The whole thing is silly. I wish *everyone* would forget it."

Her tone was sharper than she had intended, and his reply matched it. "What's eating you?" he asked, and it was as if the question had been there a long time, waiting to be asked. "Just why—why don't you want people to care about you? Is that a crime in your book?"

They stared at each other.

After a long moment of silence, Fred said, "End of conversation. Full stop. Now—how about dinner at Charlie's tonight—all the spaghetti you can eat and extra meatballs on request?"

"No thanks."

"We can discuss politics; who's going to win the pennant this year."

"Thanks anyway."

Afterward, staring at the closed door, she thought how pleasant it would have been to say yes. He was a nice fellow, fun to be with, and gentle in his way.

It was late in the afternoon before Julia had completed checking the rejection files. Nowhere had she come across handwriting like the writing in the letters. But J. Smith was there somewhere—she was sure of that.

Her secretary looked in to say good night, but Julia remained at the conference table. While going through the file, she had taken out every letter that made a reference to Mother Goose. These were stacked before her in a neat pile, ready to be checked again.

There were letters criticizing the rhythm of the old verses, and letters praising the Webster Company's two-volume edition. There were letters asking the meaning of a particular poem, or offering an explanation of another. One letter was written on stationery headed Ravensfoot Sanitarium, Belden, Colorado. It was dated February eleventh. Julia found it quite moving.

Dear Editor: I am sending you my original Modern Mother Goose Rhymes for Modern Children. *During my illness I have passed many hours making up these little poems which, I feel, would have appeal for today's child. I am allowed to sit up for a half hour every day, and during that time I have written the poems by hand. I don't mention this to gain sympathy, but to show you how very earnestly I feel about the value of the verses. Thank you for your consideration.*

The letter was signed *Dorothy Kesselman*. A note indicated that a standard printed rejection letter had been sent out on February sixteenth.

Julia picked up the phone. "Will you get me the Ravensfoot Sanitarium in Belden, Colorado, please?" she asked the late-hours operator. "I want to speak to the doctor who is caring for Dorothy Kesselman."

A few moments later, the operator called her back. Julia listened without comment to what the operator said. Then Julia thanked her and asked her to call Detective Schwarz at the police station.

"This is Julia Martell," she said when the lieutenant answered. "I think I have something for you to look into. A Dorothy Kesselman sent us some original Mother Goose nursery rhymes two months ago, and we returned them with our standard rejection letter. She was ill with advanced tuberculosis, it seems, and she died the day she received the letter. The hospital in Colorado where she was a patient says her husband, Adolph, moved to this city after his wife's death."

Without question, it was spring when Julia got off the bus that night and walked up the block. In front of the old brick house near the corner, a forsythia was in bloom. Julia looked at the narrow windows of the houses and wondered about the people behind them. Were they happy? Were they lonely? Had any of them ever noticed her as she returned night after night?

At the drugstore, Julia collected a paper, some magazines, and her medicine, which was wrapped and waiting for her.

"How are you tonight?" Julia asked the cashier, and was aware that the woman stared in surprise at the greeting. "It's spring," Julia added, foolishly.

Outside again, she headed swiftly toward her apartment. Once in the building, she tried to pass the mailbox without looking into it. But she could not ignore the white envelope, seen through the little slot in the box.

Dear Miss Peep-Peep, the letter said. *I don't know if you are much of a swimmer or a mountain climber, but it doesn't matter. The name fits—or will soon. This is my last contribution, one which you have earned by your sympathy, your compassion, and your understanding. Sincerely, J. Smith.*

Julia read it again. Then she rang for the elevator and rode upstairs. She crossed the corridor with a slow, gliding step, one designed to reveal any invisible obstacles. When she opened the door, she stood back a moment before going inside.

It could be anything this time. She had never heard of Peep-Peep.

The living room appeared as she had left it. She looked around the rest of the apartment, then with her coat still on, she took her *Complete Works of Mother Goose* from the shelf and thumbed through the index. There it was—a short riddle-rhyme about a star:

I have a little sister, they call her Peep-Peep;
She wades the waters deep, deep, deep;
She climbs the mountains high, high, high;
Poor little creature, she has but one eye.

The telephone rang. Julia picked it up and heard the voice of Lieutenant Schwarz.

"You can relax, Miss Martell," he said. "We've got your joker. Picked him up right after you called us. The husband of the Mrs. Kesselman who wrote you—he admitted it right away. Went off the deep end after his wife died. He says she worked for six months on the poems she sent you, and you didn't even . . . Well, he seems to think that if you'd sent a word of encouragement instead of a form letter, it would have made a difference. She was practically staying alive for your answer, according to him, and when it came—she just gave up."

Julia leaned back. "Yes," she said, "I understand you, Lieutenant. But it wasn't fair, was it? I mean, to put all that responsibility on me . . ."

The lieutenant sounded uncomfortable. "He says he wrote a letter that should have tipped you off," he said. "He knew he was going to be caught at this, but he didn't care . . . I'm sorry, Miss Martell. Anyway, you don't have to worry anymore."

"Do I know him?"

"Could be." Lieutenant Schwarz seemed relieved to get off the delicate subject of motive. "At least, you've seen him. He's the pharmacist in the drugstore just down the block from your place."

Julia returned the receiver to its hook and sat for a moment without moving.

> Now it's time for YOU to be The Reader as Detective.
>
> Think about the information Julia just received. Then think about the last riddle-rhyme. What trap do you think the writer planned for her. What do you think Julia did?
>
> Read on to see if you are right!

Julia picked up the bottle of eyewash from the coffee table and unwrapped it. Her handkerchief was lying on the table, and she poured a little of the liquid on the cloth. The spot widened and then, as she watched, the dampened area shredded and dissolved. Through the small round hole, she saw the wood of the coffee table turn yellow.

Poor little creature, she had but one eye.

Julia looked around the room that had been for a long time her cheerful safe retreat. Then she picked up the telephone directory and began turning pages.

"Fred," she said a moment later. "This is Julia. Are the spaghetti and meatballs still available? I think I'd like them very much."

I. The Reader as Detective

Read each question below. Then write the letter of the correct answer to each question. Remember, the symbol next to each question identifies the *kind* of reading skill that particular question helps you to develop.

1. Julia Martell worked as an

    a. artist.   *b.* editor.   *c.* office manager.

2. In the corridor near her apartment, Julia found

    a. a spider.
    b. an envelope addressed to Miss Muffet.
    c. a thin piece of gray wire.

3. The lieutenant warned Julia that the name J. Smith "was probably a pseudonym." Which expression best defines the word *pseudonym*?

    a. something bright or shiny   *c.* crazy or mad
    b. a false name

4. After Julia found a letter addressed to Miss Peep-Peep, she

    a. told Fred that she couldn't have dinner with him at Charlie's.
    b. looked up the name in her *Complete Works of Mother Goose.*
    c. called a hospital in Colorado.

5. We may infer that the eyewash Julia received at the end of the story

    a. was given to her by mistake.
    b. contained an acid or some other powerful liquid.
    c. would help her while she did hours of reading.

6. Which one of the following is *not* an opinion?

   a. Fred and Julia will probably get married one day.

   b. Mrs. Kesselman would have lived many more years if Julia had sent her an encouraging letter.

   c. The husband of Mrs. Dorothy Kesselman worked as a pharmacist in a drugstore near Julia's apartment house.

7. Julia thought she could identify the person who sent her the messages because his handwriting "was distinctive—slanting, with unfinished loops on the rising letters." What is the meaning of the word *distinctive*?

   a. very special or unusual

   b. common or ordinary

   c. delightful or amusing

8. Mr. Kesselman wanted revenge on Julia because

   a. she turned down a manuscript he sent her.

   b. he thought she contributed to the death of his wife.

   c. he was angry with her for not answering his letters.

9. At the conclusion of the story, Julia probably decided to go out with Fred because she

   a. was angry with the lieutenant.

   b. realized that he hadn't been sending her the threatening letters.

   c. made a decision to get more involved in life.

10. This story tells mainly about

   a. how Julia received threats and finally avoided getting hurt.

   b. how Julia learned about Dorothy Kesselman's death.

   c. how Julia stopped at a drugstore every evening of the week.

II. Looking at Language

A **compound word** is a word which is composed, or made up, of two smaller words. For example, *table* and *cloth* combine to form the compound word *tablecloth*. Other examples of compound words are *campfire, flashlight,* and *skyscraper.* Sometimes, you can figure out the meaning of a difficult compound word by combining the meanings of the two smaller words.

The following questions will help you find compound words when you're looking at language.

11. "Often she would reorder the eyewash that made her hours of reading possible." Which of the following words is a compound word?

a. reorder   *b.* eyewash   *c.* possible

12. "The cheerful store was especially soothing after the unpleasantness of the afternoon." Which of the following words is a compound word?

a. cheerful   *b.* unpleasantness   *c.* afternoon

13. Below are three expressions from the story. Which expression contains a compound word?

a. preferred to remain nameless
b. the same slanted handwriting
c. her own apartment building

14. Below are three sets of words found in this selection. Which group contains compound words?

a. envelope, slanting, widened
b. reminded, apartment, disbelief
c. birthday, hallway, halfway

15. In the story, the copyreaders and the secretaries pondered about Miss Muffet and her spider. The compound word *copyreaders* means

a. people who write books.
b. people who sell magazines.
c. people who read copy, or written material.

III. Finding Word Meanings

Now it's time to be a word detective. Following are ten words which appear in "The Mother Goose Madman." Study the words and their definitions. Then complete the following sentences by using each vocabulary word only *once.*

16. The first sign of the earthquake was a slight quivering, or _____ , of the ground.

17. Our school received a generous gift from an unknown person, on the condition that he or she remain _____ .

18. Please be especially careful when you wrap this gift; it is glass and is very _____ .

19. When the dog leaped out of the shadows, Ted _____ in surprise.

20. Because Camille writes so neatly and carefully, her compositions are very _____ .

21. My brother Dennis refuses to participate in any after-school activity; he is very shy and prefers to remain distant, or _____ .

22. The letter of complaint was signed by a(n) _____ employee who was displeased by the action of a supervisor.

23. When Louis realized how cold the lake was, he expressed hesitation, or _____ , at diving right in.

24. Every morning, Jennifer's mother wakes her with the _____ , "Rise and shine!"

25. When each twin claimed he was Bill, it created a rather amusing _____ .

IV. Thinking About the Case

A. Why do you think this story is called "The Mother Goose Madman"? Present evidence to support your answer.

B. As a result of what occurs in the story, Julia learned something important about herself. What did Julia learn?

C. Suppose it were possible for Julia to send a different letter of rejection to Dorothy Kesselman. What do you think Julia might say?

The Love-Philtre

by O. Henry

The Blue Light Drug Store is downtown, between the
Bowery and First Avenue, where the distance between the two streets is the shortest. The store is on a block
around which crowds of children play, and become candidates for the cough medicines and prescriptions that await
them inside.

Eddie Schipley was the night clerk of the Blue Light, and
the friend of his customers. There, as it should be, the druggist is a counselor and adviser whose learning is respected,
whose wisdom is sought after and desired.

Eddie lived at and breakfasted at Mrs. Riddle's rooming
house two blocks away. Mrs. Riddle had a daughter named
Rosy, and, as you must have guessed, Eddie adored her. She
was to the druggist the mixture, the compound, of all that
was chemically perfect and pure.

Eddie, however, was timid, and his hopes remained
grounded in fear. Behind his counter, he was confident and
dauntless; away from the store, he was weak-kneed, faint-
hearted.

Moreover, Eddie had a rival in the person of one Chunk
McGowan. Chunk was Eddie's friend and customer, and also
roomed at the Riddles'. On pleasant evenings, he often
dropped in at the Blue Light Drug Store to chat with Eddie.

One afternoon, McGowan drifted in in his silent, easy way,
and pulled up a chair.

"Eddie," said he, "listen carefully, for you may be able to
make me something I need."

Eddie looked hard at the countenance of Mr. McGowan. "What's the problem?" he asked.

Mr. McGowan smiled. "The problem is here in my heart," said Chunk. "I mean—that is—say Eddie—Rosy and me are going to run away and get married tonight."

A wild fear suddenly shook Eddie. Meanwhile, Mr. McGowan's smile began to steadily fade.

"That is," he continued, "if she doesn't change her mind when the time comes. We've been making plans for the big event for the past two weeks. One day she says she will; the next evening she says no. We've agreed on tonight, and Rosy's stuck to it now for two whole days. But there are still five hours to go, and I'm afraid she'll back down."

"You said there was something I could make for you," remarked Eddie.

Mr. McGowan looked ill at ease, a condition unusual for him. He tapped his fingers nervously against the side of the chair.

"I wouldn't have this go wrong for anything," he said. "I've rented an apartment uptown, with tulips on the table and a kettle ready to boil. And I've hired a preacher who's waiting for us to be at his house at 9:30 sharp. It's got to come off! Now if only Rosy won't change her mind again!" Mr. McGowan paused, a victim of doubts.

"I don't see yet," said Eddie shortly, "what it is I can help you with, or what I can be doing about it."

"Old man Riddle doesn't like me a bit," went on the uneasy suitor. "For a week, he hasn't let Rosy step outside the door with me. If they weren't worried about losing me as a boarder, they'd have bounced me out long ago. But I'm making a pretty fair salary, and she'll never regret flyin' the coop with Chunk McGowan."

"If you will excuse me, Chunk," said Eddie, "I must make a prescription that is to be called for soon."

"Say," said McGowan, looking up suddenly, "say Eddie, isn't there a powder of some kind, some kind of love powder, that'll make a girl like you for sure if you give it to her?"

Eddie's lip curled with scorn at the thought of such a ridiculous idea. But before he could answer, McGowan continued.

"I thought," went on Chunk, hopefully, "that if I had one

of them powders to give Rosy when I see her at supper tonight, it might keep her from backing down on the proposition to skip. I guess she doesn't need a team of mules to drag
her away, but I'd feel better if I had a little something extra
goin' for me."

Strong and simple was Chunk McGowan. A better reader
of men than Eddie could have seen that his tough frame was
strung upon fine wires. Like a good general in foreign terri-
tory, he was seeking to guard every point against possible
failure.

"When is this foolishness of running away supposed to
happen?" asked Eddie.

"Nine o'clock," said Mr. McGowan. "Supper's at seven. At
eight, Rosy says she's going to bed with a headache. At nine,
old Parvenzano lets me through to his backyard. There's a
board off Riddle's fence next door. I go under her window and
help her down the fire escape. We've got to get out early because of the preacher. It's all dead easy if Rosy doesn't balk
when the time comes. Can you fix me one of them powders,
Eddie?"

"Chunk," said he, "for drugs of that nature a pharmacist
must have much care. To you alone of my acquaintances
would I entrust a powder like that. But for you I shall make
it, and you shall see how it works."

Eddie went behind the prescription desk. There he
crushed to a powder two tablets. Each contained a quarter of
a grain of morphia. To them he added a little sugar to increase the bulk, and then folded the mixture neatly in a white
paper. Taken by an adult this powder would insure several
hours of deep sleep without danger to the sleeper. This he
handed to Chunk McGowan, telling him to administer it in a
liquid if possible, and received the hearty thanks of Mr.
McGowan.

How subtle was Eddie's plan. For he next sent a messenger for Mr. Riddle and disclosed Chunk McGowan's plan for
eloping with Rosy. Mr. Riddle was a large man, and sudden
in action.

"Much obliged," he said briefly to Eddie. "My own room's
just above Rosy's. I'll just go up there myself after supper and
load the shotgun and wait. If he comes in my backyard, I'll
have a surprise waiting for him that he'll long remember."

Eddie was elated. With Rosy deep in the clutches of sleep, and with her parent armed and waiting, he felt certain that his rival soon would be out of the picture.

All night in the Blue Light Drug Store, Eddie waited for some news of the great event. But no news came.

At eight o'clock in the morning the day clerk arrived, and Eddie started hurriedly for Mrs. Riddle's to learn the outcome. Just as he stepped out of the store who but Chunk McGowan sprang across the street and grasped his hand—Chunk McGowan with a victor's smile and flushed with joy.

"Worked like a charm!" said Chunk with a grin. "Rosy hit the fire escape on time to the second, and we made it to the preacher's at 9:30 on the nose. She's up at the apartment—she cooked eggs this morning! How lucky I am. You must drop by some day and have supper with us. I've got a job down near the bridge, and that's where I'm heading for now."

"The—the—powder?" stammered Eddie.

"Oh, that stuff you gave me," said Chunk, broadening his grin. "Well, it was this way."

65

Now it's time for YOU to be The Reader as Detective.

What do you think went wrong with Eddie's plan?
What do you think Chunk McGowan did?
Read on to see if you are right!

"I sat down at the supper table last night at Riddle's, and I looked at Rosy, and I said to myself, 'Chunk, if you get this girl, get her on the square. Don't try any hocus-pocus.' So I kept the powder you gave me in my pocket. Then my eyes fell on another person present, another person who, I thought, could show his comin' son-in-law a little more affection. So I watches my chance and dumps that love powder in old man Riddle's coffee—see?"

I. The Reader as Detective

Read each question below. Then write the letter of the correct answer to each question. Remember, the symbol next to each question identifies the *kind* of reading skill that particular question helps you to develop.

1. Eddie didn't tell Rosy that he adored her because he
   a. knew she loved Chunk.
   b. was too timid.
   c. was scared of Mr. Riddle.

2. Chunk was afraid that Rosy would
   a. marry Eddie.
   b. tell her father about their plans.
   c. change her mind about marrying him.

3. The title of this selection is "The Love-Philtre." Think about the story. Then select the expression that best defines the word *philtre*.
   a. drug or magic formula   *c.* friend or adviser
   b. store or shop

4. Which happened last?

  a. Chunk invited Eddie to have supper with Rosy and him.
  b. Chunk put the powder in Mr. Riddle's coffee.
  c. Eddie sent a messenger for Mr. Riddle.

5. Chunk told Eddie, "The problem is here in my heart." By this he meant that he

  a. had a disease of the heart.
  b. was in love.
  c. was too frightened to ask Rosy to marry him.

6. Which one of the following statements expresses an opinion?

  a. Mr. Riddle didn't like Chunk McGowan.
  b. Rosy and Chunk will probably be happy forever.
  c. Eddie lived at Mrs. Riddle's rooming house.

7. We may infer that Mr. Riddle didn't stop Chunk from running away with Rosy because he

  a. didn't believe what Eddie had told him.
  b. changed his mind about Chunk.
  c. was asleep.

8. Eddie's plan for stopping Chunk was very "subtle." What is the meaning of the word *subtle*?

  a. sly or tricky
  b. impossible to carry out
  c. huge or enormous

9. The author states that Mr. McGowan's "tough frame was strung upon fine wires." This suggests that although McGowan was powerful, he was also

  a. silly or foolish.
  b. nervous or tense.
  c. very poor.

10. This story is mainly about

  a. the life of a night clerk in the Blue Light Drug Store.
  b. how a young man succeeded in marrying the girl he loved.
  c. how Eddie waited all night for news about what had happened to Chunk.

II. Looking at Language

Synonyms are words that have the same or nearly the same meanings. For example, the words *throw* and *toss* are synonyms. The words *large*, *enormous*, and *huge* are synonyms, too. Authors use synonyms to make their writing more interesting. And by using synonyms it is possible to obtain a precise, or exact, shade of meaning.

The following questions refer to synonyms.

11. Eddie adored Rosy. A synonym for *adored* is

    a. loved.   *c.* feared.
    b. hated.

For practice, write a synonym of your own for *adored.*

12. Eddie's lip "curled with scorn at the thought of such a ridiculous idea." Which one of the following is a synonym for *ridiculous?*

    a. perfect   *c.* silly
    b. charming

For practice, write a synonym of your own for *ridiculous.*

13. Following are three expressions found in the story. Which expression contains synonyms?

    a. perfect and pure
    b. a counselor and adviser
    c. strong and simple

14. Eddie "started hurriedly for Mrs. Riddle's to learn the outcome." A synonym for *hurriedly* is

    a. sharply.   *c.* slowly.
    b. quickly.

For practice, write a synonym of your own for *hurriedly.*

15. Below are three sets of words found in the story. Which group contains synonyms?

    a. timid, weak-kneed, fainthearted
    b. friend, rival, customer
    c. unusual, confident, grasped

III. Finding Word Meanings

Now it's time to be a word detective. Below are ten words which appear in "The Love-Philtre." Study the words and their definitions. Then complete the following sentences by using each vocabulary word only *once*.

		page
dauntless	bold; fearless	62
countenance	appearance, especially the expression of the face	63
proposition	a plan or idea offered for acceptance	64
balk	to stop short and refuse to continue	64
entrust	to give over to another for protection or care	64
insure	to make sure of or certain; to protect	64
administer	to manage or supervise	64
subtle	not obvious; very clever	64
disclosed	made known; told	64
elated	filled with joy	65

16. The final page of the mystery revealed, or _____ , who the murderer was.

17. When we heard the good news, we were so _____ our joy knew no bounds.

18. On screen he is brave and _____ , but in real life he is actually quite cautious.

19. We could tell by her sad look and unhappy _____ that she had received bad news.

20. The committee presented a[n] _____ which everyone hoped the council would accept.

21. Select as a leader someone who follows things through, a person who does not _____ when the going gets rough.

22. In her new job, Consuela must _____ , or direct, a training program for new employees.

23. Eating well and exercising regularly cannot _____ you of a long life, but they will make you a healthier person.

24. Don't tell me what you want for your birthday; just give me a[n] _____hint.

25. I have such confidence in your honesty, I would _____ you with my most valued possessions.

IV. Thinking About the Case

A. Do you think Eddie did the right thing in attempting to prevent Chunk from marrying Rosy? Explain your answer.

B. Suppose Chunk hadn't put the powder in Mr. Riddle's coffee. How do you think the story would have ended?

C. Suppose you were making a movie based on "The Love-Philtre." What actor would you select for the role of Chunk? What actress do you think should play the part of Rosy? Explain your choices.

Lucky Seven

by Isaac Asimov

The thing is, Dad doesn't keep me up to date on his cases. You wouldn't expect him to. He's a detective on the police force, and I'm just finishing junior high school.

In the last couple of years, I have helped out Dad a few times when I managed to figure out a few clues. I guess that has irritated him a bit, but I plan to be a detective myself some day, and this has been good training for me. Still, Dad says he doesn't want me to dull my fine edge by exposing it too often too soon (maybe he's being a little sarcastic there), and I do try to stay in line.

So it was none of my business when Mrs. Halperin came to see him the day after her husband was arrested. I just happened to be in the next room, doing my homework, and I stayed there; so I heard.

I think Mrs. Halperin must have known Dad years back, when he was maybe no older than I was. I guessed that from the way she talked, and the way she called Dad "Joe."

Dad sounded uncomfortable. "I can't do anything, Mrs. Halperin. You know that. All the evidence makes it look as though he took that stamp."

"But if he did, Joe, he did it for me. We're getting old, and he's not well. Almost all we'll have to live on is social security, and often, that's not enough. He thinks that even if he goes to jail, I can get the stamp and sell it and have enough for a few years anyway."

Dad sounded more uncomfortable than ever. "I still can't

do anything, Mrs. Halperin. Even if that's why he did it, it's still against the law."

"But I don't want him in jail, Joe. We'll get along on social security somehow. I don't want extra money if it means being without him. What if I give back the stamp? Won't that count in his favor?"

"If the stamp is returned—considering his age, the state of his health, and his clean record till now—I think it *would* help him. I can't guarantee it, but I think it would. Have you got the stamp with you?"

"No, I don't know where it is, but he tried to tell me. Remember when you arrested him just outside the theater?"

"I tried to do it without fuss . . ."

"I know. Thank you, Joe. But he must have seen you, you see. He went into the lobby to buy gum. He chews it all the time, since he gave up smoking. He must have seen you waiting. When he came back, he was all tense, but he wouldn't say what was wrong. He thought you just might be waiting for some other reason, I suppose, and he didn't want me to find out what he had done.

"Then when we came out, and you moved toward him, he whispered to me, 'Seven, Alice, like in the old clock.' Then you had your hand on his elbow, and he went off with you. It wasn't until hours later I found out what he was supposed to have done—stolen this rare stamp from his boss."

"Do you think he was telling you where he had put the stamp, Mrs. Halperin?"

"I think so. I guess he thought I would understand, but I'm not as smart as he thinks. If you can tell where it is, though, from what I've said, and if you find it, isn't it the same as my returning it to you? And won't that help poor Sam?"

Dad said, "Do you have an old clock? Do you suppose he put it there?"

"We had an old grandfather's clock many years ago, but it's long since gone. The only other clock in the house is a new electric clock we just bought."

"And seven doesn't mean anything to you? Is there something in your house that has a seven on it, or is associated with seven?"

"I can't think of anything. Besides, he is such a cautious man. I would think he would carry it with him."

"Believe me, he was searched thoroughly, and he didn't have it."

Mrs. Halperin started to cry, and I tried to think just as quickly as I could. Suppose Mr. Halperin *was* carrying it with him. In that case, when he saw Dad waiting to arrest him, he would have to get rid of it, if he were going to save it for his wife.

Maybe he left it on his seat. But where would that seat be? Were there ticket stubs? It's the man who usually hands the tickets to the usher at the door, so Mrs. Halperin wouldn't have them. Probably she wouldn't remember the seats exactly without the stubs.

That must be what Mr. Halperin was trying to tell her, only not straight out because someone might hear. But what would "seven" mean all by itself?

It all went through my mind in a flash, and I didn't wait to hear anymore.

I left the apartment quiet as anything, and ran down the stairs. I knew the theater where Dad had made the arrest and it wasn't too many blocks from our place. I didn't have any money for a taxi, and I couldn't bear to wait for a bus, but I'm a pretty good runner.

When I got there, it was just about 9 P.M. The lobby was lit up, and the play was about to start. I tried to walk in, but the man at the door said, "Got a ticket?"

I twisted my face like I was going to cry and said, "My dad's in there. I got to find him. We got terrible trouble at home."

He couldn't stop me when I said that, and I ran down the aisle to the row I wanted. I was pretty breathless by then, but I said, "Pardon me, pardon me . . ."

Everyone stood up to let me through, even though no one could see any empty seats. I got to the seat I wanted, and there was a man sitting in it.

I whispered anxiously, "Mister, can I look under the seat? I think my mother might have left her keys there."

He got up at once, and the seat moved up with him. I could see in the dim light there was nothing on the floor and nothing attached to the bottom of the seat. I felt around to make sure.

That left only one thing. I felt under the armrest—and

there it was: a little envelope, stuck there with a wad of chewing gum, all the way back where people don't put their hands, usually.

I peeled it off, with the chewing gum, ran back up the aisle, shouted, "thanks!" to the fellow at the door and ran all the way home. I could hardly talk when I got there, and Mrs. Halperin was still there—just getting ready to leave.

All I could say was, "Here it is!" Then I just sat down and puffed.

Dad got rid of the gum, took the stamp out of the envelope and stared at it. He waited for me to catch my breath and said, "Where did you get this, Larry?" Mrs. Halperin had started to cry.

I gasped, "In the theater. Ran there."

"You were listening?"

"Doing homework, next room. Couldn't help it."

Dad said, "Where in the theater? Seventh row, seventh seat?"

"No, Dad." My breath was coming easier. "Where Mr. and Mrs. Halperin were sitting—under the armrest."

"How did you know where they were sitting?"

> Now it's time for YOU to be the Reader as Detective.
>
> How *did* Larry know where they were sitting? [Hint: Think back to the clue that Mr. Halperin gave his wife]. Now read on to see if you are right!

"I figured it had to be the 11th seat in row five, and it was. You know—VII—like the Roman numeral for seven, like an old-fashioned grandfather's clock. Lucky seven, I guess."

Dad's lip grew tighter. He said, "Why didn't you tell me?"

"No time, Dad. I was afraid it would fall and be swept up or someone would come across it and throw it away. I was so sorry for Mrs. Halperin, I couldn't waste *one minute.*"

Dad said, "Larry, it's all right to be softhearted, but when you take things into your own hands . . ."

Then he looked at Mrs. Halperin, and he squeezed my arm. His voice changed, and he said, "Never mind, Larry, you go on being softhearted."

And Mrs. Halperin kissed me.

I. The Reader as Detective

Read each question below. Then write the letter of the correct answer to each question. Remember, the symbol next to each question identifies the *kind* of reading skill that particular question helps you to develop.

1. According to Mrs. Halperin, her husband took the stamp

   a. because he needed some extra cash for a business deal.

   b. because he had been stealing things for the past several years.

   c. to get some extra money to help her in her old age.

2. Which one of the following is *not* true?

   a. Larry's dad always kept Larry up to date on his cases.

   b. Mrs. Halperin no longer had the old grandfather's clock.

   c. Larry thought that Mrs. Halperin knew his dad years ago.

3. Mr. Halperin "went into the lobby" of the theater. As used in this sentence, what is the meaning of the word *lobby?*

   a. a group of people who attempt to influence lawmakers

   b. a hall or waiting room in a building

   c. a curve or arch

4. Larry told the man at the door of the theater that he

   a. had to look for a rare stamp that was stolen.

   b. had to find his dad because there was trouble at home.

   c. had left some keys on a seat.

5. Which happened last?

   a. Larry overheard his dad talking to Mrs. Halperin.
   b. The man at the theater asked to see Larry's ticket.
   c. Mr. Halperin said, "Seven, Alice, like in the old clock."

6. Which one of the following statements expresses a fact rather than an opinion?

   a. Mr. Halperin should be sent to prison for stealing the stamp.
   b. Probably, Larry will change his mind about becoming a detective.
   c. Since Mr. Halperin gave up smoking, he chews gum all the time.

7. The stamp was found

   a. on the floor of the theater.
   b. on the bottom of the seat.
   c. stuck under an armrest.

8. How did the number VII tell Larry where the stamp was?

   a. He figured out that it was in the seventh row, seventh seat.
   b. He figured the number V meant row five; the number II meant seat eleven.
   c. He asked the man at the door to show him seat number VII.

9. Larry thought that his dad was being "a little sarcastic" when he joked about how often Larry became involved in his cases. Which of the following expressions best defines the word *sarcastic*?

   a. in a sneering or joking manner
   b. in a sorrowful way
   c. thoughtless or careless

10. Suppose this story appeared as a newspaper article. Which of the following would make the best headline?

   a. Detective's Son Discovers Stolen Stamp
   b. Suspect in Stamp Case Saved
   c. Stolen Stamp Spotted in Shop

II. Looking at Language

As you know, synonyms are words that have the same or nearly the same meanings. **Antonyms**, on the other hand, are words which have *opposite* meanings. Some examples of antonyms: *always–never, up–down, near–far.*

The following questions will give you practice in identifying antonyms.

11. When Mr. Halperin saw the detective waiting, he came back "all tense." An antonym for tense is

    a. nervous.   *b.* eager.   *c.* calm.

For practice, write an antonym for *tense.* (Note: one possibility is *relaxed.* Think of another.)

12. According to Larry, "Dad sounded more uncomfortable than ever." Which one of the following is an antonym for uncomfortable?

    a. unpleasant   *b.* at ease   *c.* interested

13. In the dim light Larry could see there was nothing on the floor. Which one of the following is *not* an antonym for dim?

    a. dull   *b.* clear   *c.* bright

14. Larry thought that Mrs. Halperin "wouldn't remember" where the seats were without the stubs. An antonym for *remember* is

    a. know.   *b.* realize.   *c.* forget.

15. Below are three pairs of words found in the story. Which pair contains antonyms?

    a. quickly, swiftly   *b.* old, new   *c.* find, look

For practice, make up a pair of antonyms of your own.

III. Finding Word Meanings

Now it's time to be a word detective. Following are five vocabulary words which appear in "Lucky Seven," and five *new* vocabulary words for you to learn. Study the words and their definitions.

Then complete the following sentences by using each vocabulary word only *once.*

		page
irritated	annoyed; bothered	71
guarantee	a pledge or promise that something will be done	72
associated	connected with or joined	72
usher	a doorkeeper, or one who shows people to their seats; to guide or show	73
numeral	a figure or word that stands for a number	75
stamina	endurance; strength	
remit	to send money	
jovial	full of fun; very merry	
brawl	a noisy quarrel or fight; to quarrel or fight	
drab	dull	

16. The vacuum cleaner comes with a two-year _____ which covers all parts and labor.

17. To receive a poster, just _____five dollars along with your name and address.

18. The Roman _____for fifteen is XV.

19. These walls look very faded and _____ ; what they need is a fresh coat of paint.

20. The umpire pretended that he was not bothered by the constant booing of the crowd, but it actually _____him very much.

21. The _____showed us to our seats and gave us programs.

22. For more than one hundred years, the names Sherlock Holmes and Doctor Watson have been closely linked, or _____ .

23. Andrea can run five miles without getting the slightest bit tired; she has excellent _____ .

24. Although no one could say who started the fight, everyone agreed it was a terrible _____ .

25. At the circus, the jolly and _____clowns kept us roaring with laughter at their tricks.

IV. Thinking About the Case

A. Suppose that Mr. Halperin had said, "*Twelve*, Alice, like in the old clock." In what row and seat would the stamp have been hidden? Explain how you figured out the answer.

B. According to Larry, he didn't tell his dad where he thought the stamp was because he "couldn't waste one minute." Think of some other reasons why Larry might not have told his dad. Explain.

C. Suppose that Larry hadn't found the missing stamp. How do you think the story would have ended?

The Force of Luck

by Rudolfo A. Anaya and José Griego y Maestas

Once two wealthy friends got into a heated argument. One said that it was money which made a man prosperous, and the other maintained that it wasn't money, but luck. They argued for some time and finally decided that if they could find an honorable man, then perhaps they could prove their respective points of view.

One day while they were passing through a small village they came upon a miller who was grinding corn and wheat. They paused to ask the man how he ran his business. The miller replied that he worked for a master and that he earned only four bits* a day, and with that he had to support a family of five.

The friends were surprised. "Do you mean to tell us you can maintain a family of five on only fifteen dollars a month?" one asked.

"I live modestly to make ends meet," the humble miller replied.

The two friends privately agreed that if they put this man to a test perhaps they could resolve their argument.

"I am going to make you an offer," one of them said to the miller. "I will give you two hundred dollars and you may do whatever you want with the money."

"But why would you give me this money when you've just met me?" the miller asked.

---

*four bits: fifty cents

"Well, my good man, my friend and I have a long-standing argument. He contends that it is luck which elevates a man to high position, and I say it is money. By giving you this money perhaps we can settle our argument. Here, take it, and do with it what you want!"

When the day's work was done, the miller decided the first thing he would do would be to buy food for his family. He took out ten dollars and wrapped the rest of the money in a cloth and put the bundle in his bag. Then he went to the market and bought supplies and meat to take home.

On the way home he was attacked by a hawk that had smelled the meat which the miller carried. The miller fought off the bird but in the struggle he lost the bundle of money. Before the miller knew what was happening the hawk grabbed the bag and flew away with it. When he realized what had happened he fell into deep thought.

"Ah," he moaned, "now I'm in the same poverty as before! And worse, because now those two men will say I am a thief! I should have thought carefully and bought nothing. Yes, I should have gone straight home and this wouldn't have happened!"

So he gathered what was left of his provisions and continued home, and when he arrived he told his family the entire story.

When he was finished telling his story his wife said, "It has been our lot to be poor, but maybe someday our luck will change."

Three months after he had lost the money to the hawk, it happened that the two wealthy men returned to the village. As soon as they saw the miller they approached him to ask if his luck had changed. When the miller saw them he felt ashamed and afraid that they would think that he had squandered the money on worthless things. But he decided to tell them the truth and as soon as they had greeted each other he told his story. The men believed him. In fact, the one who insisted that it was money and not luck which made a man prosper took out another two hundred dollars and gave it to the miller.

"Let's try again," he said, "and let's see what happens this time."

The miller didn't know what to think. "Kind sir, maybe it would be better if you put this money in the hands of another man," he said.

"No," the man insisted. "I want to give it to you because you are an honest man, and if we are going to settle our argument you have to take the money!"

The miller thanked them and promised to do his best. Then as soon as the two men left he began to think what to do with the money so that it wouldn't disappear as it had the first time. The thing to do was to take the money straight home. He took out ten dollars, wrapped the rest in a cloth, and headed home.

When he arrived his wife wasn't at home. At first, he didn't know what to do with the money. He went to the pantry where he had stored a large earthenware jar filled with bran. That was as safe a place as any to hide the money, he thought, so he emptied out the grain and put the bundle of money at the bottom of the jar, then covered it up with the grain. Satisfied that the money was safe he returned to work.

That afternoon when he arrived home from work he was greeted by his wife.

"Look, my husband, today I bought some good clay with which to whitewash the entire house."

"And how did you buy the clay if we don't have any money?" he asked.

"Well, the man who was selling the clay was willing to trade for jewelry, money, or anything of value," she said. "The only thing we had of value was the jar full of bran, so I traded it for the clay. Isn't it wonderful, I think we have enough clay to whitewash these two rooms!"

The man groaned and pulled his hair.

"What have you done? We're ruined again!"

"But why?" she asked, unable to understand his anguish.

"Today I met the same two friends who gave me the two hundred dollars three months ago," he explained, "and after I told them how I lost the money they gave me another two hundred. And I, to make sure the money was safe, came home and hid it inside the jar of bran—the same jar you have traded for dirt! Now we're as poor as we were before! And what am I going to tell the two men? They'll think I'm a liar and a thief for sure!"

"Let them think what they want," his wife said calmly.

So the miller was consoled and the next day he went to work as usual. Time came and went, and one day the two wealthy friends returned to ask the miller how he had done with the second two hundred dollars. When the poor miller saw them he was afraid they would accuse him of being a liar and a spendthrift. But he decided to be truthful and as soon as they had greeted each other he told them what had happened to the money.

"That is why poor men remain honest," the man who had given him the money said, "because they don't have money they can't get into trouble. But I find your stories hard to believe. I think you gambled and lost the money. That's why you're telling us these wild stories.

"Either way," he continued, "I still believe that it is money and not luck which makes a man prosper."

"Well, you certainly didn't prove your point by giving the money to this poor miller," his friend reminded him. "Good evening, you luckless man," he said to the miller.

"Thank you, friends," the miller said.

"Oh, by the way, here is a worthless piece of lead I've been carrying around. Maybe you can use it for something," said the man who believed in luck. Then the two men left, still debating their points of view on life.

Since the lead was practically worthless, the miller thought nothing of it and put it in his jacket pocket. He forgot all about it until he arrived home. When he threw his jacket on a chair he heard a thump and he remembered the piece of lead. He took it out of the pocket and threw it under the table. Later that night after the family had eaten and gone to bed, they heard a knock at the door.

"Who is it? What do you want?" the miller asked.

"It's me, your neighbor," a voice answered. The miller recognized the fisherman's wife. "My husband sent me to ask you if you have any lead you can spare. He is going fishing tomorrow and he needs the lead to weight down the nets."

The miller remembered the lead he had thrown under the table. He got up, found it, and gave it to the woman.

"Thank you very much, neighbor," the woman said. "I promise you the first fish my husband catches will be yours."

"Think nothing of it," the miller said and returned to bed. The next day he got up and went to work without thinking any more of the incident. But in the afternoon when he returned home he found his wife cooking a big fish for dinner.

"Since when are we so well off we can afford fish for supper?" he asked his wife.

"Don't you remember that our neighbor promised us the first fish her husband caught?" his wife reminded him. "Well this was the fish he caught the first time he threw his net. So it's ours, and it's a beauty. But you should have been here when I gutted him! I found a large piece of glass in his stomach!"

"And what did you do with it?"

"Oh, I gave it to the children to play with," she shrugged.

When the miller saw the piece of glass he noticed it shone so brightly it appeared to illuminate the room, but because he knew nothing about jewels he didn't realize its value and left it to the children. But the bright glass was such a novelty that the children were soon fighting over it and raising a terrible fuss.

Now it so happened that the miller and his wife had other neighbors who were jewelers. The following morning when the miller had gone to work the jeweler's wife visited the miller's wife to complain about all the noise her children had made.

"We couldn't get any sleep last night," she moaned.

"I know, and I'm sorry, but you know how it is with a large family," the miller's wife explained. "Yesterday we found a beautiful piece of glass and I gave it to my youngest one to play with and when the others tried to take it from him he raised a storm."

The jeweler's wife took interest. "Won't you show me that piece of glass?" she asked.

"But of course. Here it is."

"Ah, yes, it's a pretty piece of glass. Where did you find it?"

"Our neighbor gave us a fish yesterday and, when I was cleaning it, I found the glass in its stomach."

"Why don't you let me take it home for just a moment. You see, I have one just like it and I want to compare them."

"Yes, why not? Take it," answered the miller's wife.

So the jeweler's wife ran off with the glass to show it to her husband. When the jeweler saw the glass he instantly knew it was one of the finest diamonds he had ever seen.

"It's a diamond!" he exclaimed.

"I thought so," his wife nodded eagerly. "What shall we do?"

"Go tell the neighbor we'll give her fifty dollars for it, but don't tell her it's a diamond!"

"No, no," his wife chuckled, "of course not." She ran to her neighbor's house. "Ah yes, we have one exactly like this," she told the miller's wife. "My husband is willing to buy it for fifty dollars—only so we can have a pair, you understand."

"I can't sell it," the miller's wife answered. "You will have to wait until my husband returns from work."

That evening when the miller came home from work his

wife told him about the offer the jeweler had made for the piece of glass.

"But why would they offer fifty dollars for a worthless piece of glass?" the miller wondered aloud. Before his wife could answer they were interrupted by the jeweler's wife.

"What do you say, neighbor, will you take fifty dollars for the glass?" she asked.

"No, that's not enough," the miller said cautiously. "Offer more."

"I'll give you fifty thousand!" the jeweler's wife blurted out.

"A little bit more," the miller replied.

"Impossible!" the jeweler's wife cried, "I can't offer any more without consulting my husband." She ran off to tell her husband how the bartering was going, and he told her he was prepared to pay a hundred thousand dollars to acquire the diamond.

He handed her seventy-five thousand dollars and said, "Take this and tell him that tomorrow, as soon as I open my shop, he'll have the rest."

When the miller heard the offer and saw the money he couldn't believe his eyes. He imagined the jeweler's wife was jesting with him, but it was a true offer and he received the hundred thousand dollars for the diamond. The miller had never seen so much money, but he still didn't quite trust the jeweler.

"I don't know about this money," he confided to his wife. "Maybe the jeweler plans to accuse us of robbing him and thus get it back."

"Oh no," his wife assured him, "the money is ours. We sold the diamond fair and square—we didn't rob anyone."

"I think I'll still go to work tomorrow," the miller said. "Who knows, something might happen and the money will disappear, then we would be without money and work. Then how would we live?"

So he went to work the next day, and all day he thought about how he could use the money. When he returned home that afternoon his wife asked him what he had decided to do with their new fortune.

"I think I will start my own mill," he answered, "like the

one I operate for my master. Once I set up my business we'll see how our luck changes."

The next day he set about buying everything he needed to establish his mill and to build a new home. Soon he had everything going.

Six months had passed, more or less, since he had seen the two men who had given him the four hundred dollars and the piece of lead. He was eager to see them again and to tell them how the piece of lead had changed his luck and made him wealthy.

Time passed and the miller prospered. His business grew and he even built a summer cottage where he could take his family on vacation. He had many employees who worked for him. One day while he was at his store he saw his two benefactors riding by. He rushed out into the street to greet them and asked them to come in. He was overjoyed to see them, and he was happy to see that they admired his store.

"Tell us the truth," the man who had given him the four hundred dollars said. "You used that money to set up this business."

The miller swore he hadn't, and he told them how he had given the piece of lead to his neighbor and how the fisherman had in return given him a fish with a very large diamond in its stomach. And he told them how he had sold the diamond.

"And that's how I acquired this business and many other things I want to show you," he said. "But it's time to eat. Let's eat first then I'll show you everything I have now."

The men agreed, but one of them still doubted the miller's story. So they ate and then the miller had three horses saddled and they rode out to see his summer home. The cabin was on the other side of the river where the mountains were cool and beautiful. When they arrived the men admired the place very much. It was such a peaceful place that they rode all afternoon through the forest. During their ride they came upon a tall pine tree.

"What is that on top of the tree?" one of them asked.

"That's the nest of a hawk," the miller replied.

"I have never seen one; I would like to take a closer look at it!"

"Of course," the miller said, and he ordered a servant to climb the tree and bring down the nest so his friend could see how it was built. When the hawk's nest was on the ground they examined it carefully.

> Now it's time for YOU to be The Reader as Detective.
>
> What do you think the miller found in the nest? Read on to see if you are right!

They noticed that there was a cloth bag at the bottom of the nest. When the miller saw the bag he immediately knew that it was the very same bag he had lost to the hawk which fought him for the meat years ago.

"You won't believe me, friends, but this is the very same bag in which I put the first two hundred dollars you gave me," he told them.

"If it's the same bag," the man who had doubted him said, "then the money you said the hawk took should be there."

"No doubt about that," the miller said. "Let's see what we find."

The three of them examined the old weatherbeaten bag. Although it was full of holes and crumbling, when they tore it apart they found the money intact. The two men remembered what the miller had told them and they agreed he was an honest and honorable man. Still, the man who had given him the money wasn't satisfied. He wondered what had really happened to the second two hundred he had given the miller.

They spent the rest of the day riding in the mountains and returned very late to the house.

As he unsaddled their horses, the servant in charge of grooming and feeding the horses suddenly realized that he had no grain for them. He ran to the barn and checked, but there was no grain for the hungry horses. So he ran to the neighbor's granary and there he was able to buy a large clay jar of bran. He carried the jar home and emptied the bran into a bucket to wet it before he fed it to the horses. When he got to the bottom of the jar he noticed a large lump which turned out to be a rag covered package. He examined it and felt something inside. He immediately went to give it to his master who had been eating dinner.

"Master," he said, "look at this package which I found in an earthenware jar of grain which I just bought from our neighbor!"

> Now it's time for YOU to be The Reader as Detective again.
>
> You should be able to guess what they found in the jar.
>
> Read on and prove that you're right!

The three men carefully unraveled the cloth and found the other one hundred and ninety dollars which the miller had told them he had lost. That is how the miller proved to his friends that he was truly an honest man.

And they had to decide for themselves whether it had been luck or money which had made the miller a wealthy man!

I. The Reader as Detective

Read each question below. Then write the letter of the correct answer to each question. Remember, the symbol next to each question identifies the *kind* of reading skill that particular question helps you to develop.

 1. This story tells mainly about
   a. the unusual events that led to a miller's wealth.
   b. how a jeweler bought a diamond from a miller.
   c. how a miller's children kept neighbors awake.

2. The miller lost a bundle of money

    a. to thieves.   *b.* to a hawk.   *c.* while gambling.

3. How did the miller's wife get the clay to whitewash the house?

    a. She bought it.

    b. A neighbor gave it to her for some lead.

    c. She traded the bran for it.

4. By giving the miller some money, the two men hoped to "settle" their argument. As used in this sentence, which expression best defines the word *settle*?

    a. to live for a time in a particular place

    b. to sink or go lower

    c. to decide or agree upon

5. Probably, the man at first doubted the miller's tale of how he had acquired the business because

    a. the miller was known to be a liar.

    b. the story about finding a diamond in the stomach of a fish didn't seem very likely.

    c. the jeweler had told the man a different story.

6. In all, how much money did the jeweler pay for the diamond?

    a. fifty thousand dollars

    b. seventy-five thousand dollars

    c. a hundred thousand dollars

7. Which happened last?

    a. A neighbor promised to give the miller the first fish her husband caught.

    b. Two wealthy friends gave the miller some money.

    c. The miller found a cloth bag at the bottom of a hawk's nest.

8. The miller used the money he received from the jeweler to

    a. stop working and retire.

    b. start his own mill.

    c. rent a cabin in the mountains.

9. Which one of the following statements expresses a fact rather than an opinion?

a. The jeweler would surely have given the miller much more money for the diamond.

b. The miller built a summer cottage where he could take his family on vacation.

c. The miller will probably be poor again one day.

10. We may infer that at the conclusion of the story, the two men

a. agreed that luck had made the miller a wealthy man.

b. agreed that money had made the miller a wealthy man.

c. still could not agree whether it was luck or money which had made the miller a wealthy man.

II. Looking at Language

Often, you can figure out the meaning of a difficult or unfamiliar word by looking at the *context*—the words [and sometimes the sentences] around the word. **Context clues** will help you find the word's meaning.

As the Reader as Detective, you have already had experience in using vocabulary clues to figure out word meanings. The following questions will provide additional practice in using context clues to find the word's meaning.

11. The miller found a "jar filled with bran . . . so he emptied out the grain and put the bundle of money at the bottom." Context clues suggest that the word *bran* means

a. jar.

b. grain.

c. bundle.

12. When the miller saw the piece of glass "he noticed it shone so brightly it appeared to illuminate the room." By using context clues, you can figure out that *illuminate* means

a. light up.

b. cut deep.

c. darken.

13. "'I'll give you fifty thousand!' the jeweler's wife blurted out." Look at the context. Then select the expression that defines the word *blurted*.

    a. asked or questioned

    b. said suddenly without thinking

    c. to have information or know

14. The two men were debating about whether it was luck or money which made a man successful. Context clues suggest that the word *debating* means

    a. arguing.   *c.* remaining silent.

    b. playing a game.

15. When the miller learned that the money was gone, he groaned and pulled his hair in anguish. Consider the context. Then define the word *anguish*.

    a. wonder or thought   *c.* great pain or distress

    b. power or strength

III. Finding Word Meanings

Now it's time to be a word detective. Below are ten words which appear in "The Force of Luck." Study the words and their definitions. Then complete the following sentences by using each vocabulary word only *once*.

		page
prosperous	successful; doing well	81
respective	belonging to each; particular	81
contends	declares to be true	82
elevates	raises	82
provisions	a supply of food and drink	82
consoled	comforted; eased the grief of	84
spendthrift	a person who is wasteful with money	84
novelty	something fresh or unusual; newness	86
benefactors	people who give money or help to others	88
intact	untouched; whole or complete	89

16. When we packed for our camping trip, we took plenty of _____ , so that we would have enough to eat and drink.

17. As soon as my brother earns some money, he wastes it foolishly; he is a(n) _____ .

18. When I see fresh flowers on the table in a restaurant, it always lifts, or _____ , my opinion of the place.

19. When his family first came to this country, they were poor and struggling; today they are very _____ .

20. When her cat was lost, there was no way Maria could be cheered up or _____ .

21. Fortunately, my wallet was returned with nothing missing; everything was _____ .

22. Pat claims that the best baseball player who ever lived was Babe Ruth, but Fran _____ that it was Ty Cobb.

23. When Doris first got a car she drove it all the time; she used it less and less as the _____ wore off.

24. The college thanked its many _____ who had supported its programs through the years.

25. First all the classes met in the auditorium; then each class left for its _____ room.

IV. Thinking About the Case

A. Do *you* believe that it was luck or money which was responsible for the miller's success? Explain your position.

B. There is evidence in the story that the miller was honest, hardworking, intelligent, and generous. Show how these qualities also contributed to the miller's success.

C. Sometimes a story presents a lesson, or moral. What lesson or moral can be drawn from "The Force of Luck"?

"I've heard folks say you're not too good about paying what you owe them. Now, I'm not going to spend my time building you a fireplace when I'm not going to get paid for it."

A Trick of the Trade

by Dorothy S. Pratt

John Birney took his right hand from his pocket and knocked on Ard Welton's door. Nine-year-old Ada answered.

"Is your father at home, Ada?"

"Yes, Mr. Birney. Just a minute and I'll get him for you." Leaving the door ajar, she disappeared into the darkness of the living room. Several minutes later, Ard Welton appeared.

"What's your business, Birney?"

"Well, Mr. Welton, fact is, I'm needing me a fireplace for the house I just built out on Carter Road. Was wondering if you could build it for me."

Welton leaned against the door frame and crossed his arms over his chest. He raised his right hand to his chin and rubbed it thoughtfully.

"Being truthful, Birney, I've heard folks say you're not too good about paying what you owe them. Now, I'm not going to spend my time building you a fireplace when I'm not going to get paid for it."

"Folks don't have no business talking that way about me. Why, what with Elsie and the five children, money just gets tight sometimes, that's all. I might pay a little bit slow now and then, but I always pay. Besides, it's getting near October and the nights are getting chilly already. My family needs that fireplace. And folks do say you're the best durn mason in Plymouth." He shoved his hands into his coat pockets and looked hopefully at Welton.

Welton looked back at him. His hand returned to his chin. Sure as he was born, Ard had heard from many a reputable man that Birney was real slow about paying his bills, when he bothered to pay them at all. And him with a good decent-paying job down at Seth Thomas! Folks said he squandered most of his pay, and they did work for Birney only for the sake of his children and Elsie, who was a decent enough type.

"Fact is, Birney, the job would cost you a hundred dollars. Now, I'll be needing half of that before I do the job, and the other half the day I'm finished. Won't do it any other way."

"Sounds good to me, Mr. Welton. I can come up with the money. When can you do the job?"

"Oh, I suppose I can start work next Monday, and I'll be over tomorrow to take a look at what you want done. Just remember—you be there Monday at seven in the morning with fifty dollars in your hand, or that fireplace won't get started."

"OK, Mr. Welton, sounds good. I'll be there with the fifty dollars." He stuck out his right hand.

Welton took it briefly in his own. "OK, Birney. Good night now." He closed the door.

The following Monday morning, Ard drove his wagon up to the new Birney place at seven sharp. Sure enough, Birney was waiting for him, and walked up to the wagon as it came to a halt.

"Morning, Mr. Welton. Nice day."

"Morning, Birney. Got the money?"

"Well, Mr. Welton, fact is, I just couldn't get the whole fifty dollars up in so short a time. I've got forty dollars, though. Won't that be OK?"

Ard closed one eye and rubbed his chin. "Forty, eh?"

"I promise I'll have the other sixty dollars when you're finished! Please, Mr. Welton, it's awful important we get that fireplace in—I'm moving the family into the place in two weeks."

"Oh, give me the forty dollars, Birney. I'll build your fireplace, but you better have that sixty dollars the day I'm done."

Birney smiled and dug into his trouser pocket, coming up

with four worn bills, and placed them one by one into Welton's outstretched hand. "I appreciate your good heart, Mr. Welton."

Ard put the money into his deep shirt pocket, jumped nimbly off the wagon, and went to work. Between that job and some surveying he was doing for the town, it took him nearly two weeks to finish. He sent word to Birney that he expected to see him on Monday morning at the new house.

He had laid the last stone and was cleaning up when he saw Birney walking towards him. "Morning, Birney. Work's done."

"So I see. You do good work, Mr. Welton."

"That'll be sixty dollars."

Birney did not look at Ard. His eyes were glued to his brand-new chimney. "Well, Mr. Welton, fact is, I don't have it. Only worked a few days this week and. . ."

Ard didn't stay around to hear the rest. He picked up his tools, walked calmly to his wagon, climbed in, and drove away.

"Well," Birney said to himself, "that was a lot easier than I thought it would be. Welton's not as tough as everyone says he is." He laughed out loud at his own cleverness. "Nope. Welton thinks he's a smart guy, but nobody gets one by old John Birney."

Two days later, he moved his family into the new house. After the furniture was in, he decided to light a fire in his new fireplace. He put a dry log in and lit the kindling. Slowly, it burst into flame.

"Looks good, don't it, Elsie? Hey, wait a minute—why's it so smoky in here? Smoke's not going up the chimney! Elsie, get me some water—got to put that fire out quick!" He did so, and ran outside to join his wife, coughing like a sick man. When the smoke had cleared a bit, he went back inside and opened the windows. "That Welton," he muttered to himself. "Thinks he's such a good mason."

An hour later, the room once again filled with fresh air, Birney went inside. He looked up the chimney and saw nothing but the sky. "I'm going over to South Street to see Welton," he told Elsie. "Who does he think he is, building me a fireplace that don't work?"

This time, when Birney knocked on his door, Ard opened

it himself. He didn't look a bit surprised to see Birney standing there, and waited for him to speak.

"Your fireplace don't work."

"Don't work, eh?"

"That's right. I just lit it, and the smoke wouldn't go up the chimney. Why, Elsie and I nearly died."

"Look pretty healthy to me, Birney."

"Don't get smart with me, Welton. What's the matter with that fireplace?"

Ard stroked his chin and squinted at Birney. "Well, can't say that I know, Birney. I guess a man just can't expect much from a forty-dollar fireplace these days."

Birney opened his mouth but said nothing.

"You come up with sixty dollars, and I'll come down and take a look, but not a minute sooner."

"But Mr. Welton, we moved in today. We need that fireplace tonight. My poor little children are going to freeze to death!"

"Sixty dollars," said Ard, closing the door in Birney's face.

Two nights later, Birney once again knocked on the Welton door, and it was once again opened by Ard.

"I got your sixty dollars, Welton."

"Let's see it."

Birney dug the wad out of his pocket and slapped it into Ard's hand. Ard unrolled it and counted it. Twice.

"Yep, that's the sixty dollars you owe me all right." He started to close the door.

Birney put a hand up to keep it from closing. "Now wait a minute! When you coming over to fix my fireplace?"

"Your fireplace? Oh, that's right—you claim your fireplace needs fixing. Well, can't make it tomorrow—I got a wedding and some surveying to do. I'll be over Sunday afternoon after dinner. Be there around two o'clock." He closed the door before Birney could answer.

Sunday afternoon at two-thirty, Welton drove up to the new Birney place. John Birney came outside to meet him.

"Afternoon, Birney. Family home?"

"Afternoon, Mr. Welton. Nope, they're all over at Elsie's folks having Sunday dinner."

Ard jumped off his wagon. He took out a ladder and a brick

and walked to the house. Setting the ladder against the house, he quickly ascended to the roof, brick in hand.

Now it's time for YOU to be The Reader as Detective.

What do you think Ard Welton did when he built the fireplace? What is he going to do *now*? [Hint: Think about the *brick*—and the fact that Ard didn't seem particularly worried when Birney didn't pay him.]

Read on to see if you are right!

He walked up to the newly built chimney and looked down the shaft. Lifting the brick, he dropped it down the chimney, shattering the pane of glass he had mortared in so firmly the week before.

I. The Reader as Detective

Read each question below. Then write the letter of the correct answer to each question. Remember, the symbol next to each question identifies the *kind* of reading skill that particular question helps you to develop.

1. Ard Welton had heard that John Birney

    a. always paid his bills promptly.

    b. never paid his bills.

    c. paid his bills late, when he paid them at all.

2. Ard told Birney that the fireplace would cost

    a. forty dollars.   *c.* one hundred dollars.

    b. sixty dollars.

3. Ard set the ladder against the house and "quickly ascended to the roof." Which of the following expressions best defines the word *ascended?*

    a. came down or lowered

    b. rose or climbed

    c. bent or leaned

4. We may infer that Ard

    a. suspected all along that Birney would be unwilling to pay him the full amount.

    b. was eager to repair Birney's fireplace.

    c. was willing to do the job for less money than he had asked.

5. Which happened first?

    a. Birney complained to Ard that the fireplace didn't work.

    b. Birney gave Ard forty dollars.

    c. Birney thought to himself that Ard wasn't as tough as everyone said.

6. When Birney said that he didn't have the rest of the money, Ard

    a. became very angry, and started shouting.

    b. walked calmly to his wagon and drove away.

    c. said that he was going to tear down the fireplace.

7. Which one of the following statements expresses a fact rather than an opinion.

    a. It is much easier to build a fireplace than it is to paint the outside of a house.

    b. People who cheat others usually get away with it.

    c. It took Welton nearly two weeks to finish the fire-place.

8. The reason that the smoke didn't go up the chimney was

    a. the fire wasn't strong enough.

    b. the pane of glass held it back.

    c. the chimney was too long.

9. Birney stated that with five children, money sometimes got "tight." As used in this sentence, what is the meaning of the word *tight?*

    a. packed firmly   *c.* scarce

    b. strict or severe

10. This story tells mainly about

    a. how a worker used a trick to obtain the money he was owed.

    b. how some children nearly froze to death when a fire-place didn't work.

    c. the life of a man who needed a fireplace for his new house.

II. Looking at Language

Homophones are words that *sound* alike, but have different spellings and different meanings. For example, the words *weigh* and *way* are homophones. As you can tell, they are pronounced the same, but they are spelled differently and have different meanings. Some other homophones are *mail* and *male,* as well as *eight* and *ate.* Because homophones are similar, they are often confused. Therefore, it is important to be able to recognize them when you're looking at language.

The following questions will provide practice in identifying homophones.

11. John Birney "took his right hand from his pocket and knocked on Ard Welton's door." A homophone for *right* is

 a. ride.
 b. wrote.
 c. write.

12. Ard dropped the brick, "shattering the pane of glass." Which one of the following words is a homophone for *pane*?

 a. paid
 b. pain
 c. panel

13. Following are three pairs of words found in the story. Which pair contains homophones?

 a. don't, done
 b. for, four
 c. night, tight

14. Below are three pairs of words found in the story. Which pair does *not* contain examples of homophones?

 a. know, no
 b. two, to
 c. took, look

15. On Sunday afternoon, John Birney came outside to meet Ard. A homophone for *meet* is

 a. meat.
 b. met.
 c. team.

III. Finding Word Meanings

Now it's time to be a word detective. Listed below are five vocabulary words which appear in "A Trick of the Trade," and five *new* vocabulary words for you to learn. Study the words and their definitions. Then complete the following sentences by using each vocabulary word only *once*.

		page
ajar	slightly open	95
reputable	well thought of; honorable	96
squandered	spent foolishly; wasted	96
mason	a person who works with brick and stone	97
mortar	a mixture of cement, sand, lime, and water used for holding stones or bricks together	99
decomposed	rotten; broken apart	
recommendation	a suggestion	
duration	length of time	
logical	reasonable; of good sense and reason	
reinforce	to strengthen	

16. During the long, icy winter, the old stone grill partially collapsed and became badly _____ .

17. Please close the door completely; if you leave it _____ , the cat will run out.

18. To make your essay stronger, give some examples to _____ , or support, your point of view.

19. The solution to the problem seemed so practical and _____ , we wondered why we had not thought of it before.

20. Did you know that the _____ of the Hundred Years War was actually more than a century?

21. That company does excellent work and is completely reliable; it is very _____ .

22. By making several foolish business deals, she quickly _____ her fortune.

23. Several bricks in the fireplace are loose; by applying some _____ we can easily make the repair.

24. Now is the time to suggest candidates for class president; do you have a _____ ?

25. After the electrician and the carpenter left, the _____ began to work on the chimney.

IV. Thinking About the Case

A. Why do you think this story is called "A Trick of the Trade"? Do you believe Ard Welton knew of, or used, this "trick" before—or did he think of it just for this occasion? Explain your answer.

B. When Birney finally paid Ard the sixty dollars, Ard counted it—twice. What does this tell us about the character of Ard Welton? About John Birney? Birney thought that Ard was "not as tough" as people made him out to be. Did this prove to be the case? Explain, giving examples.

C. The last time that John Birney knocked on Ard Welton's door, Ard "didn't look a bit surprised to see Birney standing there." Explain why. Think of one reason why Birney might have decided not to complain to Welton after all.

Thank You, M'am

by Langston Hughes

She was a large woman with a large purse that had everything in it but hammer and nails. It had a long strap and she carried it slung across her shoulder. It was about eleven o'clock at night, and she was walking alone, when a boy ran up behind her and tried to snatch her purse. The strap broke with the single tug the boy gave it from behind. But the boy's weight, and the weight of the purse combined caused him to lose his balance so, instead of taking off full blast as he had hoped, the boy fell on his back on the sidewalk, and his legs flew up. The large woman simply turned around and kicked him right square in his blue-jeaned sitter. Then she reached down, picked the boy up by his shirt front, and shook him until his teeth rattled.

After that the woman said, "Pick up my pocketbook, and give it here."

She still held him. But she bent down enough to permit him to stoop and pick up her purse. Then she said, "Now ain't you ashamed of yourself?"

Firmly gripped by his shirt front, the boy said, "Yes'm."

The woman said, "What did you want to do it for?"

The boy said, "I didn't aim to."

She said, "You a lie!"

By that time two or three people passed, stopped, turned to look, and some stood watching.

"If I turn you loose, will you run?" asked the woman.

"Yes'm," said the boy.

105

"Then I won't turn you loose," said the woman. She did not release him.

"I'm very sorry, lady, I'm sorry," whispered the boy.

"Um-hum! And your face is dirty. I got a great mind to wash your face for you. Ain't you got nobody home to tell you to wash your face?"

"No'm," said the boy.

"Then it will get washed this evening," said the large woman starting up the street, dragging the frightened boy behind her.

He looked as if he were fourteen or fifteen, frail and willow-wild, in tennis shoes and blue jeans.

The woman said, "You ought to be my son. I would teach you right from wrong. Least I can do right now is to wash your face. Are you hungry?"

"No'm," said the being-dragged boy. "I just want you to turn me loose."

"Was I bothering you when I turned that corner?" asked the woman.

"No'm."

"But you put yourself in contact with *me*," said the woman. "If you think that that contact is not going to last awhile, you got another thought coming. When I get through with you, sir, you are going to remember Mrs. Luella Bates Washington Jones."

Sweat popped out on the boy's face and he began to struggle. Mrs. Jones stopped, jerked him around in front of her, put a half nelson about his neck, and continued to drag him up the street. When she got to her door, she dragged the boy inside, down a hall, and into a large kitchenette-furnished room at the rear of the house. She switched on the light and left the door open. The boy could hear other roomers laughing and talking in the large house. Some of their doors were open, too, so he knew he and the woman were not alone. The woman still had him by the neck in the middle of her room.

She said, "What is your name?"

"Roger," answered the boy.

"Then, Roger, you go to that sink and wash your face," said the woman, whereupon she turned him loose—at last. Roger looked at the door—looked at the woman—looked at the door—*and went to the sink*.

"Let the water run until it gets warm," she said. "Here's a clean towel."

"You gonna take me to jail?" asked the boy, bending over the sink.

"Not with that face, I would not take you nowhere," said the woman. "Here I am trying to get home to cook me a bite to eat and you snatch my pocketbook! Maybe you ain't been to your supper either, late as it be. Have you?"

"There's nobody home at my house," said the boy.

"Then we'll eat," said the woman. "I believe you're hungry—or been hungry—to try to snatch my pocketbook."

"I wanted a pair of blue suede shoes," said the boy.

"Well, you didn't have to snatch *my* pocketbook to get some suede shoes," said Mrs. Luella Bates Washington Jones. "You could of asked me."

"M'am?"

The water dripping from his face, the boy looked at her. There was a long pause. A very long pause. After he had dried his face and not knowing what else to do dried it again, the boy turned around, wondering what next. The door was open. He could make a dash for it down the hall. He could run, run, run, run, *run*!

The woman was sitting on the daybed. After a while she said, "I were young once and I wanted things I could not get."

There was another long pause. The boy's mouth opened. Then he frowned, but not knowing he frowned.

The woman said, "Um-hum! You thought I was going to say *but*, didn't you? You thought I was going to say, *but I didn't snatch people's pocketbooks*. Well, I wasn't going to say that." Pause. Silence. "I have done things, too, which I would not tell you, son—neither tell God, if he didn't already know. So you set down while I fix us something to eat. You might run that comb through your hair so you will look presentable."

In another corner of the room behind a screen was a gas plate and an icebox. Mrs. Jones got up and went behind the screen. The woman did not watch the boy to see if he was going to run now, nor did she watch her purse which she left behind her on the daybed. But the boy took care to sit on the far side of the room where he thought she could easily see him out of the corner of her eye, if she wanted to. He did not trust the woman *not* to trust him. And he did not want to be mistrusted now.

"Do you need somebody to go to the store," asked the boy, "maybe to get some milk or something?"

"Don't believe I do," said the woman, "unless you just want sweet milk yourself. I was going to make cocoa out of this canned milk I got here."

"That will be fine," said the boy.

She heated some lima beans and ham she had in the icebox, made the cocoa, and set the table. The woman did not ask the boy anything about where he lived, or his folks, or anything else that would embarrass him. Instead, as they ate, she told him about her job in a hotel beauty shop that stayed open late, what the work was like, and how all kinds of women came in and out, blonds, redheads, and brunettes. Then she cut him a half of her ten-cent cake.

"Eat some more, son," she said.

When they were finished eating, she got up and said,

Now it's time for YOU to be The Reader as Detective.

What do you think Mrs. Jones told Roger? [Hint: Think about the kind of person Mrs. Jones is.]
Read on to see if you are right!

"Now, here, take this ten dollars and buy yourself some blue suede shoes. And next time, do not make the mistake of latching onto *my* pocketbook *nor anybody else's*—because shoes come by devilish ways like that will burn your feet. I got to get my rest now. But I wish you would behave yourself, son, from here on in."

She led him down the hall to the front door and opened it. "Goodnight! Behave yourself!" she said, looking out into the street.

The boy wanted to say something else other than, "Thank you, m'am," to Mrs. Luella Bates Washington Jones, but he couldn't do so as he turned at the barren stoop and looked back at the large woman in the door. He barely managed to say, "Thank you," before she shut the door. And he never saw her again.

I. The Reader as Detective

Read each question below. Then write the letter of the correct answer to each question. Remember, the symbol next to each question identifies the *kind* of reading skill that particular question helps you to develop.

1. Roger said he wanted to steal the purse in order to
   a. buy food.   c. buy a new shirt.
   b. buy new shoes.

2. Which one of the following is *not* true.
   a. Mrs. Jones gave Roger ten dollars.
   b. Mrs. Jones ordered Roger to wash his face.
   c. Roger made a dash for the door and began to run.

3. We may infer that Mrs. Jones was
   a. afraid of Roger.
   b. a caring person who had high principles.
   c. very wealthy.

4. Mrs. Jones "put a half nelson about his neck, and continued to drag him up the street." A *half nelson* is
   a. a wrestling hold.
   b. a piece of jewelry.
   c. a short-sleeved shirt.

5. Which happened last?
   a. Mrs. Jones gave Roger ten dollars.
   b. Mrs. Jones grabbed Roger by the front of his shirt.
   c. Roger asked if he should go to the store.

6. Mrs. Jones said that if Roger were her son she would
   a. get him a good job.
   b. give him plenty of money.
   c. teach him right from wrong.

7. Which one of the following statements expresses an opinion?

    a. Mrs. Jones should definitely have turned Roger over to the police.

    b. Roger said that there was nobody at home at his house.

    c. Mrs. Jones told Roger about her job in a hotel beauty shop.

8. As a result of the incident with Mrs. Jones, Roger probably

    a. entered a life of crime.

    b. became a good friend of Mrs. Jones.

    c. learned a lesson he never forgot.

9. Mrs. Jones told Roger that he might "run that comb through your hair so you will look presentable." Which expression best defines the word *presentable*?

    a. much older

    b. able to give a gift

    c. fit to be seen

10. Which of the following morals best expresses a main idea in this story?

    a. To err is human, to forgive, divine.

    b. Absence makes the heart grow fonder.

    c. Waste not, want not.

II. Looking at Language

As you know, an adjective is a word that describes a noun, and a verb is a word that shows action. The following questions will help you review adjectives and verbs when you are looking at language.

11. Mrs. Jones "reached down, pulled the boy up by his shirt front, and shook him until his teeth rattled." Which pair of words does *not* contain verbs?

    a. reached, pulled

    b. until, front

    c. shook, rattled

12. ''Then it will get washed this evening,'' said the large woman starting up the street, dragging the frightened boy behind her. Identify the pair of adjectives.

    a. get, washed   *c.* evening, woman
    b. large, frightened

13. Mrs. Jones dragged Roger into the room, switched on the light, and left the door open. The words *dragged*, *switched*, and *left* are

    a. synonyms.   *b.* adjectives.   *c.* verbs.

14. Roger was a slender youth with a dirty face. The words *slender* and *dirty* are

    a. adjectives.   *b.* verbs.   *c.* antonyms.

15. Identify the sentence which contains a verb *and* an adjective.

    a. The boy fell on the sidewalk.
    b. Was I bothering you when I turned the corner?
    c. The embarrassed boy dried his face.

III. Finding Word Meanings

Now it's time to be a word detective. Listed below are five vocabulary words which appear in ''Thank You, M'am,'' and five *new* vocabulary words for you to learn. Study the words and their definitions. Then complete the following sentences by using each vocabulary word only *once*.

		page
slung	thrown	105
frail	weak	106
suede	a soft leather, or leather-like fabric	108
mistrusted	doubted; failed to believe	109
latching	holding onto	109
irks	bothers; annoys	
dredge	to dig up	
uproar	a condition of loud noise and confusion	
itemize	to list unit by unit	
dilute	to weaken; make thinner	

16. For weeks after his illness, he remained pale, weak, and
_____ .

17. Perhaps you should take an umbrella, for if it rains your new
_____coat will be ruined.

18. She saved herself from drowning by _____onto the
side of the boat until help arrived.

19. The detective managed to _____ , or unearth, many
facts about the witness's past.

20. When a fire broke out in the theater, there was a deafening
_____ , as people everywhere tried to rush desperately
to safety.

21. To weaken the acid, add a quart of water; that will _____
the solution.

22. Shortly before closing time, the store manager checks the re-
ceipts and begins to _____each article that was sold
during the day.

23. Nothing _____me more than having someone honk
the horn the second the light turns green; it's very annoying.

24. A person who is known to be a liar is bound to be _____ .

25. She started on the hike with a smile on her face and a backpack
_____over her shoulder.

IV. Thinking About the Case

A. What evidence is there in the story that Roger respected Mrs.
Jones and wanted her to like him?

B. Why do you think Mrs. Jones gave Roger the ten dollars? Do
you agree with her decision? Explain.

C. Suppose that Roger and Mrs. Jones met each other five years
later. What do you think Roger might have said to Mrs. Jones?

You Can't Take It with You

by Eva-Lis Wuorio

There was no denying two facts. Uncle Basil was rich. Uncle Basil was a miser.

The family were unanimous about that. They had used up all the words as their temper and their need of ready money dictated. Gentle Aunt Clotilda, who wanted a new string of pearls because the one she had was getting old, had merely called him Scrooge Basil. Percival had declared Uncle Basil a skinflint, miser, tightwad, with colorful adjectives added. The rest had used up all the other words in the dictionary.

"He doesn't have to be parsimonious,* that's true, with all he has," said Percival's mother. "But you shouldn't use rude words, Percival. They might get back to him."

"He can't take it with him," said Percival's sister Letitia, combing her golden hair. "I need a new fur but he said, 'Why? It's summer.' Well!"

"He can't take it with him" was a phrase the family used so often it began to slip out in front of Uncle Basil as well.

"You can't take it with you, Uncle Basil," they said. "Why don't you buy a sensible house out in the country, and we could all come and visit you? Horses. A swimming pool. The lot. Think what fun you'd have, and you can certainly afford it. You can't take it with you, you know."

Uncle Basil had heard all the words they called him be-

---

*parsimonious: miserly

cause he wasn't as deaf as he made out. He knew he was a stingy, penny-pinching hoarder and curmudgeon* (just to start with). There were other words, less gentle, he'd also heard himself called. He didn't mind. What galled him was the often-repeated warning, "You can't take it with you." After all, it was all his.

He'd gone to the Transvaal† when there was still gold to be found if one knew where to look. He'd found it. They said he'd come back too old to enjoy his fortune. What did they know? He enjoyed simply having a fortune. He enjoyed also saying no to them all. They were like circus animals, he often thought, behind the bars of their thousand demands of something for nothing.

Only once had he said yes. That was when his sister asked him to take on Verner, her somewhat slow-witted eldest son. "He'll do as your secretary," his sister Maud had said. Verner didn't do at all as a secretary, but since all he wanted to be happy was to be told what to do, Uncle Basil let him stick around as an all-around handyman.

Uncle Basil lived neatly in a house very much too small for his money, the family said, in an unfashionable suburb. It was precisely like the house where he had been born. Verner looked after the small garden, fetched the papers, and filed his nails when he had time. He had nice nails. He never said to Uncle Basil, "You can't take it with you," because it didn't occur to him.

Uncle Basil also used Verner to run messages to the bank, and such, since he didn't believe in the mails or the telephone. Verner got used to carrying thick envelopes back and forth without ever bothering to question what was in them. Uncle Basil's lawyers, accountants, and bank managers also got used to his somewhat unorthodox‡ business methods. He did have a fortune, and he kept making money with his investments. Rich men have always been allowed their foibles.

Another foible of Uncle Basil's was that, while he still was in excellent health, he had Verner drive him out to an old-fashioned carpenter shop, where he had himself measured for a coffin. He wanted it roomy, he said.

---

*curmudgeon: a bad-tempered and difficult person
†Transvaal: a province, or division, of the Republic of South Africa
‡unorthodox: unusual

The master carpenter was a dour countryman of the same generation as Uncle Basil, and he accepted the order matter-of-factly. They consulted about woods and prices, and settled on a medium-price, unlined coffin. A lined one would have cost double.

"I'll line it myself," Uncle Basil said. "Or Verner can. There's plenty of time. I don't intend to pop off tomorrow. It would give the family too much satisfaction. I like enjoying my fortune."

Then one morning, while in good humor and sound mind, he sent Verner for his lawyer. The family got to hear about this, and there were in-fights, out-fights, and general quarreling while they tried to find out to whom Uncle Basil had decided to leave his money. To put them out of their misery, he said, he'd tell them the truth. He didn't like scattering money about. He liked it in a lump sum. Quit bothering him about it.

That happened a good decade before the morning his housekeeper, taking him his tea, found him peacefully asleep forever. It had been a good decade for him. The family hadn't dared to worry him, and his investments had risen steadily.

Percival, always pressed for money, had threatened to put arsenic in his tea, but when the usual proceedings were gone through, Uncle Basil was found to have died a natural death. "A happy death," said the family. "He hadn't suffered."

They began to remember loudly how nice they'd been to

him and argued about who had been the nicest. It was true too. They had been attentive, the way families tend to be to rich and stubborn elderly relatives. They didn't know he'd heard all they'd said out of his hearing, as well as the flattering drivel they'd spread like soft butter on hot toast in his hearing. Everyone, recalling his own efforts to be thoroughly nice, was certain that he and only he would be the heir to the Lump Sum.

They rushed to consult the lawyer. He said that he had been instructed by Uncle Basil in sane and precise terms. The cremation was to take place immediately after the death, and they would find the coffin ready in the garden shed. Verner would know where it was.

"Nothing else?"

"Well," said the lawyer in the way lawyers have, "he left instructions for a funeral repast. Everything of the best. Goose and turkey, venison and beef, oysters and lobsters. He liked to think of a good send-off, curmudgeon though he was, he'd said."

The family was a little shaken by the use of the word "curmudgeon." How did Uncle Basil know about that? But they were relieved to hear that the lawyer also had an envelope, the contents of which he did not know, to read to them at the feast after the cremation.

They all bought expensive black clothes, since black was the color of that season anyway, and whoever inherited would share the wealth. That was only fair.

Only Verner said that couldn't they buy Uncle Basil a smarter coffin? The one in the garden shed was pretty tatty, since the roof leaked. But the family hardly listened to him. After all, it would only be burned, so what did it matter?

So, duly and with proper sorrow, Uncle Basil was cremated.

The family returned to the little house as the housekeeper was leaving. Uncle Basil had given her a generous amount of cash, telling her how to place it so as to have a fair income for life.

They were a little surprised, but not dismayed, to hear from Verner that the house was now in his name. Uncle Basil had also given him a small sum of cash and told him how to invest it. The family taxed* him about it, but the amount was so nominal they were relieved to know Verner would be off their hands. Verner himself, though mildly missing the old man because he was used to him, was quite content with his lot. He wasn't used to much, so he didn't need much.

The storm broke when the lawyer finally opened the envelope.

There was only one line in Uncle Basil's scrawl.

"I did take it with me."

Of course there was a great to-do. What about the fortune? The millions and millions!

Yes, said the men of affairs, the accountants, and even the bank managers, who finally admitted, yes, there had been a very considerable fortune. Uncle Basil, however, had drawn large sums in cash, steadily and regularly, over the past decade. What had he done with it? That the men of affairs, the accountants, and the bank managers did not know. After all, it had been Uncle Basil's money, his affair.

Not a trace of the vast fortune ever came to light.

> Now it's time for YOU to be The Reader as Detective.
>
> What happened to Uncle Basil's fortune? Think about Uncle Basil's *last words*—and about the clues in the story. Then answer this question.
> Read on to see if you are right!

No one thought to ask Verner, and it didn't occur to Verner to volunteer that for quite a long time he had been lining the coffin, at Uncle Basil's behest, with thick envelopes he brought back from the banks. First he'd done a thick layer of these envelopes all around the sides and bottom of the coffin. Then, as Uncle Basil wanted, he'd tacked on blue cloth.

He might not be so bright in his head but he was smart with his hands.

He'd done a neat job.

---

*taxed: blamed or accused

I. The Reader as Detective

Read each question below. Then write the letter of the correct answer to each question. Remember, the symbol next to each question identifies the *kind* of reading skill that particular question helps you to develop.

1. Which statement is true of Uncle Basil?

   a. He owned horses and a swimming pool.

   b. He loved his family very much.

   c. He became rich by finding gold.

2. What did Verner do?

   a. He gave advice to Uncle Basil about how to invest his money.

   b. He looked after the garden and ran messages.

   c. He tried to convince Uncle Basil to spend more money.

3. Probably, Uncle Basil ordered a "roomy" coffin because he

   a. wanted to make sure that there was enough room for the envelopes.

   b. wanted to make a good impression on his family.

   c. was an unusually large person.

4. Percival called Uncle Basil a "skinflint and a miser." Which expression best defines the word *skinflint*?

   a. a very thin person

   b. a very cheap or stingy person

   c. a person who gets into accidents often

5. Which happened last?

   a. Uncle Basil had himself measured for a coffin.

   b. The family learned that the house had been given to Verner.

   c. Percival's sister told Uncle Basil that she needed a new fur.

6. What did Uncle Basil leave the housekeeper?

   a. nothing

   b. a small sum of money

   c. a generous amount of cash

7. Which one of the following statements expresses an opinion rather than a fact?

    a. Uncle Basil would have been much happier living in a large house in the country.

    b. Verner worked as a handyman for Uncle Basil.

    c. Over the years, Uncle Basil took large sums of money out of the bank.

8. Uncle Basil "left instructions for a funeral repast." It contained turkey, beef, and oysters. What is a repast?

    a. a meal   *c.* a joke or amusing story

    b. a past event

9. We may infer that the envelopes that lined Uncle Basil's coffin were filled with

    a. letters.   *c.* cash.

    b. business papers.

10. This story tells mainly about

    a. how Uncle Basil died.

    b. how a family made fun of a miser behind his back.

    c. how a miser managed to "take" his money with him.

II. Looking at Language

A **simile** compares two unlike things by using the words *like* or *as*. For example, each of the following sentences contains a simile:

- The frightened child was trembling like a leaf in the breeze.
- She is as graceful as a cat.

Similes—like colorful verbs and powerful adjectives—help to make language more vivid and descriptive.

The following sentences will give you practice in identifying similes.

11. Below are three descriptions of Uncle Basil's family. Which description contains a simile?

    a. They were greedy and demanding.

    b. They made fun of Uncle Basil behind his back.

    c. They behaved like circus animals.

12. Which one of the following sentences contains a simile?

  a. The family argued loudly about how nice they'd been to Uncle Basil.
  b. It seems that Uncle Basil was as sly as a fox.
  c. It looked as though Basil would live forever.

13. Uncle Basil was as stubborn

  a. as a mule.   *c.* as ever.
  b. as could be.

14. The family believed that Uncle Basil should live

  a. as comfortably as possible.
  b. in a house with a magnificent pool.
  c. like a king.

15. The family's flattering words were

  a. as pleasant as could be.
  b. like soft butter on hot toast.
  c. intended for Uncle Basil's ears.

III. Finding Word Meanings

Now it's time to be a word detective. Below are ten words which appear in "You Can't Take It with You." Study the words and their definitions. Then complete the following sentences by using each vocabulary word only *once*.

		page
unanimous	in total agreement; when everyone shares the same opinion	114
dictated	required; ordered	114
hoarder	a person who gathers and stores money, food, supplies, etc.	115
galled	annoyed; irritated	115
foible	a small fault or weak point	115
attentive	paying attention	117
drivel	silly talk; nonsense	117
sane	of sound mind	117
inherited	received from an ancestor	117
nominal	in name only; slight; not meaningful	118

16. Not one person voted against the resolution; it passed by a[n] _____ decision.

17. He is a wonderful person who has just one _____ : sometimes he talks too much.

18. The forecast for strong winds and heavy rain _____ that we take an umbrella.

19. His very superior attitude was extremely annoying; it _____ everyone.

20. The lawyer argued that the criminal was by no means crazy, but was, in fact, perfectly _____ .

21. When I arrived at the store, I discovered that all the cans of tuna fish were gone; some _____ had bought every case.

22. The money that Doreen _____ from her grandfather will help pay for her college education.

23. That is the silliest nonsense I've ever heard; I never listened to such _____ in my life.

24. Since, by law, he was not permitted to offer his services free, he charged the town the _____ fee of one dollar.

25. One reason that Charlene does so well in school is that she is very _____ ; she never misses a thing.

IV. Thinking About the Case

A. What evidence is there in the story to suggest that Uncle Basil was not as cheap as his family thought?

B. Why is the story called ''You Can't Take It with You''? How effective is this title? Explain.

C. Do you think that this story would make a good television play? Explain your answer.

Five Thousand Dollars Reward

PART 1

by Melville Davisson Post

My visitor, Walker, was a tall man with a lean face and sharp features. You might have taken him for an engineer of some sort, rather than an official in the United States Secret Service.

He placed on my desk a bulky manuscript, saying, "These are my memoirs, the account of my most unusual cases." Walker paused for a moment as his face lighted up. "But there's one case," he went on, "you won't find here." He tapped the manuscript with his finger. "It's about how I found a hobo at Atlantic City who was the best detective I ever saw."

"Why did you leave it out?"

Walker took a big gold watch out of his pocket and turned it over in his hand. On the back was an inscription. "Well," he said, still staring at the watch, "the boys in the department think quite a bit of me. I wouldn't like them to know how a dirty tramp put one over on me at Atlantic City. I don't mind telling you, but I couldn't put it in a manuscript."

"What's the story?" I asked.

Walker settled himself comfortably in the chair, and I was careful not to interrupt him.

"Well," said Walker, "I was sitting in a beach chair out there on the Boardwalk in Atlantic City in front of the Traymore Hotel. I was exhausted and had come up to Atlantic City to get a day or two of rest and sea air. The fact is, the whole department was pretty depressed. You may remember what we were up against, as it finally got into the newspapers.

"The government printing plates on the new issue of savings bonds had disappeared. We knew how they had been stolen, and we thought we knew the man who had masterminded the job. It narrowed down to Mulehaus or old Vronsky. We soon found out it wasn't Vronsky. He was in Joliet Prison. So it was Mulehaus, the way we figured it. After all, it was a job big enough for him—nothing very petty. With the government printing plates, he could print savings bonds just the way the Treasury would—and later sell them all over the world."

Walker paused and moved his gold-rimmed glasses a little higher on his nose. "I'll say this for Mulehaus. He's the hardest man to identify in the kingdom of crooks. It's more than disguises with him—false whiskers and a limp. He has the rare ability to *become* the character he pretends to be. That's the reason nobody has ever been able to track him down.

"But we did know a few things about Mulehaus, of course. He's German and had once been a sailor and a tanner. And he loves to pass himself off as a banker. He's been a French banker in Egypt, and a Swiss banker in Argentina."

Walker turned away from his digression and got back to his story. "Anyway," he said, "it was a clean job. They had got away with the plates and we didn't have a clue. We thought, naturally, that they'd make Mexico or some South American country their destination, and then start up their printing press there. So we kept the ports and borders under the tightest security. Nothing could have gotten through. All the customs officers were working with us, as well as just about every agent in the Department of Justice."

Walker paused and placed his fingers across his thin, protruding chin.

"You see the government *had* to get those plates back before the crook started to print—or else we'd have to round up every savings bond of that issue from all over the country. You can imagine what kind of job that would be.

"So we had our problems. We weren't even sure that

Mulehaus was in America. He could have been directing the job from Rio or a Mexican port. But we were certain it was Mulehaus. It was he who sold the counterfeit securities in Egypt, and he's the man who put the bogus Argentine bonds on our market.

"Well," he went on, "I was sitting out there in the beach chair, looking at the sun on the sea and thinking about the case, when I noticed this hobo that I've been talking about. He had moved round from behind me and was now leaning against the railing.

"He was a big fellow, a little stooped, unshaved and dirty. His mouth was slack and loose, and he had a big mobile nose that seemed to move about like a piece of soft rubber. His clothing was a sight. He was wearing a cap that must have been fished out of the bottom of a barrel, no shirt, just an old, drab, ragged coat, a pair of faded trousers, and tattered sneakers without socks.

"Altogether, this tramp was a sorry-looking and pathetic creature. And it occurred to me that working as a beach attendant was one job that offered employment with few questions asked.

"I suppose he saw me staring at his outfit, for he crossed one leg over the other, took a deep bow, and said with a flourish, 'Sure Governor, I ain't dolled up like a Wall Street lawyer.'

"There was a sort of arrogant unconcern about the man that gave even his miserable condition a kind of distinction. He may have been down and out, but he did not seem discouraged about it.

"'But if I had a ten-dollar bill,' he continued, 'I could really dazzle.' He looked me straight in the eye. 'Couldn't point the way to one, could you, Governor?'

"Before I could answer, he added quickly, 'I could work for it, Governor, not real work—I don't do real work—and not murder neither. Give me something to do that goes between 'em.'

"The fantastic manner of the man was amazing. 'Okay,' I said, thinking about Mulehaus, 'go out and find me a man who was once a deserter from the German army, was a tanner in Munich, and began life as a sailor, and I'll double your money—I'll give you a twenty-dollar bill.'

"The creature whistled softly. 'That's some little order,' he said.

"At that moment, a messenger from the post office came to me with the daily reports from Washington. I got out of the chair, tipped the beach attendant, and went into the hotel.

"There was nothing new from the department except that our organization over the country was in close touch. We had offered a five thousand dollars reward for the recovery of the plates, and the Post Office Department was now posting the notice all over America in every post office.

"I had forgotten about the hobo—not that I had any reliance in him—when, about five o'clock, he passed me as I strolled along the Boardwalk. He was in full stride and he had something clutched in his hand.

"He called to me as he hurried along: 'I found him, Governor. See you later!'

"'See me now,' I said. 'What's the hurry?'

"He opened his hand, revealing a shining silver dollar.

"'Can't stop now,' he said.

"I smiled at this clever and deceitful creature. He was saving me for later. He knew he could point out anyone and say he was Mulehaus, and I would gladly give him some coins to hear his story."

Walker paused. Then he went on:

"I was right. The hobo was waiting for me when I came out of the hotel the following morning.

"'Howdy, Governor,' he said. 'I located your man.'

"I was interested to hear the story he had made up to enrich himself. 'How did you find him?' I said.

"'Some luck, Governor, and some sleuthin'. It was like this. I thought you was stringin' me along. But I thought to myself I'll keep an eye out. Maybe it's on the level—anything can happen.'

"He put up his hand to emphasize his point. 'And believe it or not, Governor,' he went on, 'about four o'clock up at the other end of the Boardwalk, I passed a big, well-dressed banker-looking gent walking stiff from the hip and throwing out his leg as he walked. *Eureka!* I thought to myself. He's doin' the goosestep. Nobody but an old army man walks that way. I happened to have an empty rolling chair with me, and I went over to him.

"'Care for a chair, Admiral?' I said.

"'He looked at me sort of funny.'

"'What makes you think I'm an admiral?' he asks.

"'Well,' I say, 'nobody could be lookin' at the sea the way you do with that look of lovin' ownership unless he'd bossed her a bit. If I'm right, Admiral, you rent the chair.'

"He laughed, but he got in. 'I'm not an admiral,' he said, 'but it is true that I have followed the sea.'

"The hobo paused and threw a fist up in the air with excitement.

"'Two points, Governor—the gent had been a sailor and a soldier. Now how about the tanner business?'

"He scratched his head, moving the ridiculous cap.

"'That sort of puzzled me, and I pushed the chair along the Boardwalk thinkin' about it. If a man was a tanner, what would his markin's be?

"'I knew that tanners worked with leather. And I tried to remember everybody I'd ever seen handling leather. All at once I recollected that the first thing a shoemaker does when he picks up a piece of leather is to smooth it out with his thumbs. An' I said to myself, now that'll be what a tanner does, only he does it more . . . he's always doin' it. Then I asked myself what would be the markin's?'"

"The hobo paused, his mouth open, his head twisted to one side.

"'And right away, Governor, I got the answer to it—flat thumbs!'"

"The hobo stepped back with an air of victory.

"'And he had 'em. I asked him what time it was. I told him it was so I could tell when the hour rental for the chair was up. But the real reason was so I could see his hands.'"

Walker crossed one leg over the other.

"It was a clever story," said Walker, "and I hesitated to shatter it. But the question had to come.

"Where is the man?" I said.

"The hobo seemed a little embarrassed. 'That's the trouble, Governor,' he answered. 'He gave me a dollar to run an errand. You saw the dollar. And when I got back he was gone.'"

Walker paused. "It was a good fairytale he had told me and was worth something. I offered him half a dollar. Then I got a surprise.

"'No, Governor,' he said, 'I'm in it for the twenty-dollar bill. Where'll I find you about noon?'

"I told him where I'd be, and he started to shuffle away. But there were two things in his story that troubled me. Where did he get the silver dollar from? And how did he happen to make his imaginary man, Mulehaus, look like a banker? I'd mentioned the sailor and the tanner business, but I'd never said that Mulehaus often looked like a banker."

> Now it's time for YOU to be The Reader as Detective.
>
> How was the hobo able to find Mulehaus? Was it really Mulehaus he found? How do you think the story will end?

Try the following exercises. Then read Part 2 of "Five Thousand Dollars Reward."

I. The Reader as Detective

Read each question below. Then write the letter of the correct answer to each question. Remember, the symbol next to each question identifies the *kind* of reading skill that particular question helps you to develop.

1. Which one of the following would make the best headline for the story?

    a. Agent Tells of Pilfered Plates and Helpful Hobo
    b. Secret Service Catches Clever Crook
    c. Government Officials Guard Borders

2. Walker was sure that Mulehaus

    a. was working as a sailor.
    b. had robbed a jewelry store.
    c. had masterminded a crime at the Treasury Department.

3. Select the statement which is *not* true of Mulehaus.

    a. He was once in the German army.
    b. He often pretended to be a banker.
    c. He escaped from Joliet Prison.

4. The hobo took a deep bow and spoke "with a flourish." As used in this sentence, which expression best defines the word *flourish*?

    a. good health
    b. bold, sweeping movements
    c. a musical passage

5. We may infer that Mulehaus

    a. always worked alone.
    b. would have made an excellent actor.
    c. will probably give up his life of crime.

6. Walker was in Atlantic City because he

    a. tracked a criminal there.
    b. was trying to get some rest.
    c. lived there.

7. Which happened last?

 a. The hobo showed Walker a shiny silver dollar.

 b. A messenger gave Walker the daily reports from Washington.

 c. Walker described Mulehaus and offered the hobo twenty dollars to find him.

8. Which one of the following statements expresses an opinion rather than a fact?

 a. Mulehaus probably headed for Mexico or some South American country.

 b. The hobo was wearing a ragged coat and a pair of faded trousers.

 c. The hobo called Walker "Governor."

9. This story is called "Five Thousand Dollars Reward" because

 a. that was the sum of money that had been stolen.

 b. that was the sum offered for the return of the printing plates.

 c. that was the amount of money printed by the thieves.

10. According to the hobo, he thought that the "admiral" had been a tanner because

 a. he loved the sea.

 b. he was German.

 c. he had flat thumbs.

II. Looking at Language

As you know, it is often possible to figure out the meaning of a difficult or unfamiliar word by looking at the *context*—the words [and sometimes the sentences]—around the word. The questions below will give you additional practice in using context clues to find a word's meaning. These words may be somewhat more difficult than earlier ones. But your experience in using context clues should permit you to figure out their meaning.

11. Walker placed on the desk his memoirs, "the account of my most unusual cases." Which expression best defines the word *memoirs*?

   a. notes or letters from friends
   b. a list of expenses
   c. the story of a person's experiences

12. The criminal, Mulehaus, had sold counterfeit securities in Egypt and had passed off some "bogus" bonds in Argentina. What is the meaning of the word *bogus*?

   a. large
   b. fake
   c. perfect

13. The hobo had "a mobile nose that seemed to move about like a piece of soft rubber." Context clues suggest that the word *mobile* means

   a. capable of being moved or moving
   b. disorderly or unruly
   c. pointed or sharp

14. When the stolen plates could not be found, "the whole department was pretty depressed." As used in this sentence, what is the meaning of the word *depressed*?

   a. pressed down or lowered
   b. very sad
   c. reduced in price

15. The speaker "turned away from his digression and got back to his story." What is a *digression*?

   a. a straying away from the main subject
   b. a sum of money
   c. a type of machine

III. Finding Word Meanings

Now it's time to be a word detective. Following are ten words which appear in Part 1 of "Five Thousand Dollars Reward." Study the words and their definitions. Then complete the following sentences by using each vocabulary word only *once*.

		page
manuscript	a typewritten or handwritten copy of a book, article, or story	123
destination	the place where someone or something is headed	124
protruding	pushing or thrusting outward	124
counterfeit	false; not genuine, usually intended to deceive	125
securities	stocks, bonds, or other valuable certificates	125
pathetic	arousing pity and sympathy	125
arrogant	too proud or self-important	126
reliance	trust; confidence	126
enrich	to make more valuable	127
emphasize	to stress or give special force to	127

16. According to the pilot, we should reach our _____ in fifteen minutes.

17. Whenever he wished to accent, or _____ , a point, the speaker pounded his fist on the table.

18. In the safe were bonds, stocks, and other valuable _____.

19. My parents have always told me that a good education will _____my life.

20. Since the _____was very well-written, the editor had few changes to make.

21. The _____twenty-dollar bill was difficult to distinguish from one which was genuine.

22. The children fished from a long dock which was _____ twenty-five or thirty feet out into the sea.

23. The story was so sad, touching, and _____ , it brought tears to our eyes.

24. If James gives you his word you can count on it; I place complete _____on him.

25. Now that she is rich and famous, she is very pleased with herself and acts in a high and mighty, or _____ , manner.

IV. Thinking About the Case

A. Why was it important for the government to obtain the stolen plates as quickly as possible?

B. Although the hobo was shabbily dressed and seemed "down and out," he possessed confidence and "a kind of distinction." What other character traits did the hobo possess?

C. The hobo stated, "I don't do real work—and not murder neither. Give me something to do that goes between 'em." What did the hobo mean by this?

Five Thousand Dollars Reward

PART 2

"As I said, I'd mentioned the fact that Mulehaus had been a sailor and a tanner, but I never said that Mulehaus often looked like a banker. I didn't press the hobo on the banker business, but I did ask him where he got the silver dollar.

"'I forgot about that, Governor,' he said. 'It was like this. At the bottom of the Boardwalk, there's an old wooden fence by the road, then sand down to the sea. About halfway between the fence and the water there's a shed with some junk in it. You've seen it, I'm sure.

"'The Admiral says to me, 'Cut across back to that old shed. See if you see any automobile tracks there, and I'll give you a silver dollar.' An' I done it, an' he gave it.'

"The hobo started off. As he did, he called to me: 'Be here later, Governor, an' I'll lead you to him.'"

Walker leaned over, rested his elbows on the arms of his chair, and linked his fingers together.

"That gave me a new insight into the creature. He was a slicker article than I'd imagined. I was not to get off with just giving him a tip. No, he was taking some pains to put the touch on me for greater revenue."

Walker put out his hand and rippled the pages of the manuscript on the table. Then he went on:

134

"I was waiting for him when he came by later. I was not in a very good mood. Our plans for catching Mulehaus were just marking time. We had an agent on every ship going out of America, and we had the borders and airports covered as tight as a drum. But, so far, Mulehaus had somehow managed to elude us, and we seemed incapable of finding him. There was no sign of the fugitive. Meanwhile, the Treasury was screaming for the plates—and we didn't have a clue to where they were."

Walker stopped for a moment. Then he continued.

"'Governor,' says the hobo when he saw me later, 'you won't get mad if I say a little something?'

"'Go on and say it,' I said.

"'Well then, Governor, beggin' your pardon. You're not Mr. Henry P. Johnson from Erie. You're an agent of the United States Secret Service from Washington!'"

Walker moved restlessly in his chair.

"That made me angry," he went on, "angry at my carelessness in letting the hobo see the official letters brought to me by the post office messenger.

"'Now I'll say a little something myself,' I told him loudly, growing a little angry and belligerent. 'You discovered who I was by seeing my name on the letters. Then, later, in the post office, you saw the notice of the reward for the stolen plates. That gave you an idea of how to increase your tip. But it won't work. You won't get a cent out of me now. Because you never found any tanner—there isn't any such person.'

"The effect of my words on the hobo were even more startling than I had anticipated. His jaw dropped and he looked at me in astonishment.

"'No such person!' he exclaimed. 'Why, Governor, I found a man like that—an' he was a banker!'"

Walker put out his hands in a puzzled gesture.

"There it was again—the description of Mulehaus as a banker!"

Walker did not move, but he stopped for a moment.

"The tramp came close to me and didn't flinch for a moment. The anxiety in his face was sincere beyond question.

"'I can't find the banker man, Governor. He's flown the coop. But I believe I can find what he's hid.'

"'Well, then,' I said, 'go and find it.'

"'Now, Governor,' he whimpered, 'what good would it do me to find them plates?'

"'You'd get five thousand dollars,' I said.

"'Well, then, I've got a line on this thing, Governor,' he said. 'I've thought it all over, and this is the way it would be. They're afraid of the border, so they runs the loot down here in an automobile. They hides it in the area, and plans to get it out on one of the steamers that go by. This banker man didn't know the automobile had got here until he sent me to look, and there ain't been no steamer along since then. I've been specially careful to find that out.'

"And then the creature began to whine. 'Have a heart, Governor. Come along with me. Give me a chance!'

"I agreed, and we went directly to the bottom of the Boardwalk and then to the old shed. It was small, with a hard dirt floor made of clay and sand. All around it, from the sea to the fence, was soft sand. There were some pieces of junk and debris in the shed, but nothing of value.

"The hobo pointed out the track of a man clearly outlined in the sand. It led from the fence to the shed and then back, with no other track about.

"'Now, Governor,' he began, when he had taken a look at the tracks, 'the man that made them tracks carried something into this shed. He left it here and it was something heavy.'

"I was fairly certain that the hobo had come out earlier and made the tracks himself, but I went along with him.

"'How do you know that?' I said.

"'Well, Governor,' he answered, 'take a look at them two lines of tracks. In the one comin' to the shed the man was walkin' with his feet apart. And in the one goin' back he was walkin' with his feet in front of one another. That's because he was carryin' somethin' heavy when he came in an' nothin' when he left.'

"The hobo saw my interest and he added:

"'Did you never notice a man carryin' a heavy load? He kind of totters, walkin' with his feet apart to keep his balance. That makes his foot tracks side by side, instead of one in front of the other as he makes them when he's goin' light.''

Walker interrupted his narrative with a comment:

"It's the truth. I've verified it. A line running through the center of the heel prints of a man carrying a heavy burden will be a zigzag, while one through the heel prints of the same man without the burden will be almost straight.

"The tramp went on:

"'Whatever he brought in didn't go out, so it must be here.'

"And he began to go over the inside of the shed. He searched it like a man searching a box for a jewel. He would have found a bird's egg, but he found nothing.

"'Suppose,' I said, 'that this man wished to mislead us. Suppose that instead of bringing something here, he took something away?'

"The hobo looked at me without changing his position.

"'How could he, Governor? He was pointing this way with the load.'

"'By walking backward,' I said.

"The hobo dived out of the door and disappeared. Moments later he returned.

"'Nope, Governor,' he said. 'If a man's walkin' forward in the sand, the *toe* of his shoe digs deeper in the sand. But if he's walkin' backward his *heel* digs deeper.'

"At this point, I began to have some respect for the man's ability. He looked around the shed without moving for about a minute. Then suddenly, he snapped his fingers.

"'I got it, Governor!'

"He dashed out of the door and was gone for perhaps twenty minutes. When he returned, he came in with a bucket of water.

"'Now look, Governor,' he said, 'do I get the five thousand if I find this stuff?'

"'Certainly,' I answered him.

"'An' there'll be no foolin' around, Governor. You'll take me down to a bank yourself an' put the money in my hand?'

"'I promise you that,' I assured him.

"'Okay,' he answered, and he picked up the bucket. Beginning at the door, he poured the water carefully on the hard earth. When the bucket was empty, he brought another and another, working all the time with unusual zeal. Finally, near the middle of the floor space he stopped.

"'Here it is!' he said. 'It's buried here!'

"'Why do you think the plates are buried here?' I said.

"'Look at the air bubbles comin' up, Governor,'" he answered.

Walker stopped, and then added:

"It's a thing which I did not know until that moment, but it's the truth. If hard-packed earth is dug up and then re-packed, air gets into it, and if one pours water on the place, air bubbles will come up."

He did not go on, so I asked him, "And you found the plates there?"

"Yes," he replied, "buried in a box."

"And the hobo got the money?"

"Surely," he answered. "I put it into his hand, and let him go with it, as I promised."

Again he was silent, and I turned to him in surprise.

"Then," I said, "why did you begin this story by saying that the hobo put one over on you? I don't get it? He found the plates and he was entitled to the reward."

Walker put his hand into his pocket, took out a piece of paper, and handed it to me.

"I didn't see it either," he said, "until I got this letter."

I unfolded the letter carefully. It was neatly written and dated from Brazil.

> Now it's time for YOU to be The Reader as Detective.
>
> What do you think the letter said? Clues in the story should help you figure out the answer.
> Read on to see if you are right!

Dear Colonel Walker:

When I discovered that you were planting an agent on every ship, I had to abandon the plates and try for the reward. Thank you for the five thousand. It covered expenses.

Very sincerely yours,
D. MULEHAUS

I. The Reader as Detective

Read each question below. Then write the letter of the correct answer to each question. Remember, the symbol next to each question identifies the *kind* of reading skill that particular question helps you to develop.

1. Walker did *not* tell the hobo that Mulehaus

a. had been a sailor.
b. once worked as a tanner.
c. often looked like a banker.

2. Walker thought that the chair attendant had discovered his true identity by

a. asking questions at the hotel.
b. seeing some official letters.
c. noticing his picture at the post office.

3. According to the hobo, when a person carries a heavy load, he "kind of totters," and walks "with his feet apart to keep his balance." Which expression best defines the word *totters*?

a. marches straight ahead
b. walks unsteadily or with shaky steps
c. looks very happy

4. We may infer that Mulehaus and the hobo

    a. were the same person.

    b. were actually brothers.

    c. had never heard of each other.

5. Which happened last?

    a. The hobo poured buckets of water on the hard earth in the shed.

    b. Walker showed the publisher the letter which had been written by Mulehaus.

    c. The hobo said that the admiral asked him to look for automobile tracks in the sand.

6. Which one of the following statements expresses an opinion rather than a fact?

    a. Walker probably caught Mulehaus before too long.

    b. The plates had been buried in the sand.

    c. Walker paid the hobo five thousand dollars.

7. The conclusion of the story suggests that Mulehaus

    a. decided to confess and turn himself in.

    b. thought he could succeed in escaping with the plates.

    c. was, indeed, a master of disguises.

8. Walker thought that the hobo was trying to get "greater revenue than twenty dollars." What is the meaning of the word *revenue*?

    a. kind words or praise

    b. income or payment

    c. happiness or joy

9. The hobo stated that he got the silver dollar

    a. from Walker.

    b. from the admiral.

    c. by finding it in the sand.

10. This selection tells mainly about

    a. how Walker was tricked out of five thousand dollars.

    b. how a hobo found automobile tracks in the sand.

    c. how agents at the border failed to find Mulehaus.

II. Looking at Language

The repetition of consonant sounds is known as **alliteration**. Some examples of alliteration are:

- The *r*oad was *r*ough and *r*ugged.
- *S*ue *s*ang *s*ix *s*ongs.

Writers use alliteration to create mood and to emphasize certain words. In addition, alliteration often lends rhythm and a musical quality to language.

The questions below will give you practice in identifying alliteration.

11. Which one of the following expressions illustrates alliteration?
   a. as tight as a drum
   b. soft sand to the sea
   c. between the fence and the water

12. Each of the following sentences describes something Walker did in the story. Which sentence contains alliteration?
   a. Walker offered the beach attendant half a dollar.
   b. Walker took a piece of paper out of his pocket.
   c. Walker moved restlessly in his chair.

13. Identify the expression which illustrates alliteration.
   a. by the bottom of the boardwalk
   b. a hard dirt floor made of clay
   c. the track of a man outlined in the sand

14. Following are three sentences from the story. Which one contains alliteration?
   a. The hobo put one over on you.
   b. He was a slicker article than I'd imagined.
   c. The hobo dived out of the door and disappeared.

15. Select the sentence which does not illustrate alliteration.
   a. When he walks backward, his heel digs deeper.
   b. The printing plates were placed in a buried box.
   c. He poured the water carefully on the earth.

III. Finding Word Meanings

Now it's time to be a word detective. Below are ten words which appear in Part 2 of "Five Thousand Dollars Reward." Study the words and their definitions. Then complete the following sentences by using each vocabulary word only *once*.

		page
insight	the ability to recognize, or see into, the true nature of something	134
elude	to escape from; avoid	135
incapable	not able to	135
fugitive	one who flees or runs away, especially from the law or justice	135
belligerent	at war or warlike; in a very unfriendly and angry manner	135
flinch	to draw back suddenly with pain or surprise	135
debris	scattered ruins or remains	136
narrative	a story or description of events, real or imaginary	136
zeal	great enthusiasm	137
entitled	having a legal right or claim to something	138

16. Although it took several months, and a chase through several states, the police finally caught the _____ .

17. Both fighters demonstrated a very hostile, or _____ , attitude toward each other.

18. The person who writes the best essay is _____ to a set of books, the award for first place.

19. If someone flicks a hand toward your face, it is almost impossible not to _____ .

20. Along the shoreline we could see the scattered fragments, or _____ , of an ancient ship which had been shattered against the rocks many years ago.

21. Camille is a tireless person who approaches every job with so much energy, or _____ , she often works extra hours.

22. The eye doctor said, "Obviously you require glasses, since you are _____ of reading beyond the first line on the chart."

23. After you have studied filmmaking for some time, you may gain some special understanding, or _____ , into how directors think.

24. Your story is a truly fascinating _____ ; you should submit it to a magazine.

25. By scampering up the tree, the cat was able to avoid, or _____ , the dog.

IV. Thinking About the Case

A. At some point in the story, did you become aware that Mulehaus and the hobo were the same man? If so, when? As you review the story, what clues were there that Mulehaus and the hobo were one and the same?

B. Do you think that Walker was right in deciding not to include this story in his manuscript? Explain.

C. Would you recommend this selection to a friend? If so, explain why you enjoyed it. If not, indicate what disappointed you.

"Hector felt the blood rushing to his face and tried to control his embarrassment and anger. They should have spent the money on my shoes instead of on a dumb party, thought Hector."

Shoes for Hector

by Nicholasa Mohr

Hector's mother had gone to see Uncle Luis the day before graduation, and he had come by the same evening. Everyone sat in the living room watching Uncle Luis as he took a white box out of a brown paper bag. Opening the box, he removed a pair of shiny, light-caramel-colored shoes with tall heels and narrow, pointed toes. Holding them up proudly, he said, "Set me back 12 bucks, boy!"

Everybody looked at Hector and then back at Uncle Luis.

"Here you go, my boy . . ." He gestured toward Hector. "Try them on."

"I'm not gonna try those things on!" Hector said.

"Why not?" asked Uncle Luis. "What's wrong with them? They are the latest style, man. Listen, boy, you will be *a la moda** with these."

"They . . . they're just not my type. Besides, they don't go with my suit—it's navy blue. Those shoes are orange!" Hector's younger brothers and sister looked at each other and began to giggle and laugh.

"Shut up, you dummies!" Hector shouted angrily.

"Hector, what is the matter with you?" his mother asked. "That's no way to behave."

"I'd rather wear my sneakers than those, Mami. You and Papi promised to buy me shoes. You didn't say nothing about wearing Uncle Luis's shoes."

"Wait a minute, now. Just a minute," Hector's father said.

*a la moda: Spanish for "stylish"

144

"We know, but we just couldn't manage it now. Since your Uncle Luis has the same size foot like you, and he was nice enough to lend you his new shoes, what's the difference? We done what we could, son; you have to be satisfied."

Hector felt the blood rushing to his face and tried to control his embarrassment and anger. His parents had been preparing his graduation party now for more than a week. They should have spent the money on my shoes instead of on a dumb party, he thought. Hector had used up all the earnings from his part-time job. He had bought his suit, tie, shirt, socks, and handkerchief. His parents had promised to buy him the shoes. Not one cent left, he thought, and it was just too late now.

"It's not my fault that they lay me off for three days," his father said, "and that Petie got sick and that Georgie needed a winter jacket and Juanito some . . ."

As his father spoke, Hector wanted to say a few things. Like, No, it's my fault that you have to spend the money for shoes on a party and a cake and everything to impress the neighbors and the *familia*. Stupid dinner! But instead he remained quiet, looking down at the floor, and did not say a word.

"Hector . . . come on, my son. Hector, try them on, *bendito**. Uncle Luis was nice enough to bring them," he heard his mother plead. "Please, for me."

"Maybe I can get into Papi's shoes," Hector answered.

"My shoes don't fit you. And your brothers are all younger and smaller than you. There's nobody else. You are lucky Uncle Luis has the same size foot," his father responded.

"Okay, I'll just wear my sneakers," said Hector.

"Oh, no . . . no, never mind. You don't wear no sneakers, so that people can call us a bunch of *jíbaros*†! You wear them shoes!" his mother said.

"Mami, they are orange!" Hector responded. "And look at them pointed fronts—they go on for a mile. I'm not wearing them!"

"Come on, please," his mother coaxed. "They look nice and brand new, too."

"Hector!" his father said loudly. "Now, your Uncle Luis

---

*bendito (ben DEE toe): Spanish expression for "dear"
†jíbaros (HEE bah rose): a Puerto Rican slang word for "peasants"

was nice enough to bring them, and you are going to try them on." Everyone was silent and Hector sat sulking. His mother took the shoes from Uncle Luis and went over to Hector.

"Here, son, try them on, at least. See?" She held them up. "Look at them. They are not orange, just a light-brown color, that's all. Only a very light brown."

Without looking at anyone, Hector took the shoes and slowly put them on. No doubt about it, they felt like a perfect fit.

"How about that?" Uncle Luis smiled. "Now you look sharp. Right in style, boy!"

Hector stood up and walked a few paces. In spite of all the smiling faces in the living room, Hector still heard all the remarks he was sure his friends would make if he wore those shoes.

"Okay, you look wonderful. And it's only for one morning. You can take them right off after graduation," his mother said gently.

Hector removed the shoes and put them back in the box, resigned that there was just no way out. At that moment he even found himself wishing that he had not been selected as valedictorian and wasn't receiving any honors.

"Take your time, Hector. You don't have to give them back to me right away. Wear the shoes for the party. So you look good," he heard Uncle Luis calling out as he walked into his bedroom.

"That stupid party!" Hector whispered out loud.

With a pained expression on his face the next morning, Hector left his apartment wearing Uncle Luis's shoes. His mother and father walked proudly with him.

Hector arrived at the school auditorium and took his place on line. Smiling and waving at him, his parents sat in the audience.

"Hector López . . ." He walked up the long aisle onto the stage. He finished his speech and sat on a chair provided for him on the stage. They called his name again several times, and each time Hector received an honor or prize. Included were a wristwatch and a check for cash. Whenever Hector stood up and walked to the podium, he prayed that no one would notice his shoes.

Finally, graduation exercises were over and Hector hurried off the stage, looking for his parents. People congratulated him on his many honors and on his speech. His school friends shook his hand and they exchanged addresses. Hector found himself engaged in long good-byes. Slowly, people began to leave the large auditorium, and Hector and his parents headed for home.

Hector sat on his bed and took off Uncle Luis's shoes. "Good-bye," he said out loud, making a face, and dropped them into the box. He sighed with relief. No one had even mentioned the shoes, he thought. Man . . . I bet they didn't even notice them. Boy! Was I ever lucky . . . Nobody said a word. How about that? he said to himself. Reaching under the bed, he took out his sneakers and happily put them on. Never again, he continued, if I can help it. No, sir. I'm gonna make sure I got me shoes to wear! He remembered all the things he had won at graduation. Looking at his new wristwatch, he put it on. That's really something, he thought. He took out the check for cash he had received and read, "*Pay to the Order of Hector López . . . The Sum of Twenty-Five Dollars and 00/100 Cents.*" I can't wait to show everybody, he said to himself.

Hector left his room and looked into the kitchen. His mother and grandmother were busily preparing more food. He heard voices and music in the living room and quickly walked in that direction. When his younger brothers and sister saw him, they jumped up and down.

"Here's Hector!" Petie yelled.

"Happy Graduation Day, Hector!" everyone shouted.

The living room was full of people. His father was talking to Uncle Luis and some neighbors. Uncle Luis called out, "There he is. Hector! . . . There's my man now."

"Look." Hector's father pointed to a table that was loaded with platters of food and a large cake. The cake had the inscription "Happy Graduation to Hector." Behind the cake was a large card printed in bright colors:

HAPPY GRADUATION DAY, HECTOR
FROM ALL YOUR FAMILY
Mami, Papi, Abuelita, Petie, Georgie,
Juanito, and Millie

Rows of multicolored crepe-paper streamers were strung across the ceiling and walls. Lots of balloons had been blown up and attached to each streamer. A big bell made of bright-red crepe paper and cardboard was set up under the center ceiling light. The record player was going full blast with a loud merengue*; some of the kids were busy dancing. Hector's face flushed when he saw Gloria. He had hoped she would come to the party, and there she was. Looking great, he thought.

Some neighbors came over and congratulated Hector. His friends began to gather around, asking him lots of questions and admiring his wristwatch.

"Show them the check, Hector," his father said proudly. "That's some smart boy; he just kept getting honors! Imagine, they even give him money . . ."

Hector reached into his jacket pocket and took out the check for twenty-five dollars. He passed it around so that everyone could see it. Impressed, they asked him, "Hey, man. Hector, what you gonna do with all that money?"

"Yeah. Tell us, Hector, what you gonna do?"

> Now it's time for YOU to be The Reader as Detective.
>
> What do you think Hector is going to do with the money? You should have a good idea.
> Read on to see if you are right!

Hector smiled and shrugged his shoulders. "Buy me a pair of shoes! Any color except orange!" he replied.

---

*merengue (meh REN geh): a kind of dance

I. The Reader as Detective

Read each question below. Then write the letter of the correct answer to each question. Remember, the symbol next to each question identifies the *kind* of reading skill that particular question helps you to develop.

1. Hector didn't want to wear the shoes because

  a. they were orange.
  b. he didn't like the pointed fronts.
  c. both of the above

2. Hector used the earnings from his part-time job to

  a. buy a suit and some other clothing.
  b. buy a wristwatch.
  c. help pay for the food and cake for his graduation party.

3. We may infer that Hector

  a. was one of the very top students in his school.
  b. seldom studied.
  c. was often absent from classes.

4. Hector looked at the shoes in the box and was "resigned that there was just no way out." As used in this sentence, which expression best defines the word *resigned?*

  a. quit a job
  b. signed again
  c. forced oneself to accept a situation

5. Which happened last?

  a. Hector passed around the check for twenty-five dollars.
  b. Hector's father pointed to the graduation cake.
  c. Uncle Luis took a pair of shoes out of a brown paper bag.

6. How did Hector's parents feel about Hector?

  a. They were embarrassed that everyone in the audience was looking at his shoes.
  b. They felt that he had not done his best at school.
  c. They were very proud of him.

7. Evidence in the story suggests that Hector

   a. was disappointed with the awards he had received.
   b. liked Gloria very much.
   c. didn't make a very good speech.

8. Which one of the following statements expresses an opinion rather than a fact?

   a. Every student in the audience was extremely jealous of Hector.
   b. Hector received a wristwatch at graduation.
   c. The shoes cost Uncle Luis twelve dollars.

9. Hector hurried off the stage after the "graduation exercises." As used in this sentence, what is the meaning of the word *exercises*?

   a. activities to keep physically fit
   b. ceremonies
   c. lessons taught in school

10. This story tells mainly about

   a. how Hector argued with his parents.
   b. how some neighbors congratulated Hector.
   c. events related to Hector's graduation.

II. Looking at Language

As you know, *synonyms* are words that have the same or nearly the same meanings, while *antonyms* are words that have opposite meanings. *Homophones*, on the other hand, are words that sound alike, but have different spellings and different meanings.

The following questions will help you review synonyms, antonyms, and homophones.

11. Uncle Luis "gestured toward Hector." A synonym for *gestured* is

   a. questioned.   *b.* motioned.   *c.* smiled.

12. "You can take the shoes off right after graduation," Hector's mother said gently. Which one of the following is an antonym for *gently*?

   a. sadly   *b.* kindly   *c.* harshly

13. Hector thought that there was "not one cent left." A homophone for *cent* is

 a. tens.   *b.* scent.   *c.* penny.

14. Each of the following words appears in "Shoes For Hector." Select the pair which does *not* contain synonyms.

 a. perfect, fit   *b.* prize, honor   *c.* notice, see

15. The words below appear in the story. Identify the pair of homophones.

 a. bright, shiny
 b. one, won
 c. embarrassment, relief

III. Finding Word Meanings

Now it's time to be a word detective. Listed below are five vocabulary words which appear in "Shoes For Hector," and five *new* vocabulary words for you to learn. Study the words and their definitions. Then complete the following sentences by using each vocabulary word only *once*.

		page
responded	answered; replied	146
sulking	gloomy and bad-tempered	147
valedictorian	the student, usually ranked highest in the class, who gives the farewell speech at graduation	147
podium	a raised platform for a speaker or performer	147
streamers	long, narrow strips of paper or cloth for decoration	149
err	to make a mistake; go wrong	
doff	to remove; take off	
diminish	to make smaller; decrease	
surgeon	a doctor who performs operations	
excel	to be better than; to be superior at	

16. Ever since his error cost our team the game, Tom has been _____ ; he seems always to be in a bad mood.

17. Hanging from the ceiling were party balloons, banners, and _____ .

18. The _____who performed the operation said that the patient should recover fully in about a month.

19. Everyone at the graduation agreed that the _____delivered one of the most moving speeches in years.

20. A good way to lose weight is to reduce, or _____ , the amount of food you eat.

21. The conductor stepped to the _____and bowed to the orchestra.

22. Although it is human to _____ , or make an occasional blunder, it is not advisable to make this a habit.

23. When I asked Mr. Winthrop if I passed the test, he _____ by saying, "Just barely."

24. When the flag passes by, it is customary to _____your hat.

25. At the moment, you are only an average piano player; if you wish to _____ , you must practice much more.

IV. Thinking About the Case

A. Hector thought that his parents should have spent money for the shoes as they had promised, rather than on making a party. Do you agree? Explain.

B. The López family felt very close to each other. Present evidence from the story to support this statement.

C. Suppose that Hector hadn't used the money to buy shoes. How do you think he might have spent it? Base your answer on information found in the story?

"I tell you, guv'nor, a man who was in it don't forget about it. Last thing I ever saw was C shop going up in one grand flame, and gas pouring in all the busted windows."

A Man Who Had No Eyes

by MacKinlay Kantor

A beggar was coming down the avenue just as Mr. Parsons emerged from his hotel.

He was a blind beggar, carrying the traditional battered cane, and thumping his way before him with the cautious effort of the sightless. He was a shaggy, thick-necked fellow; his coat was greasy about the lapels and pockets, and his hand grasped the cane's crook with a futile sort of clinging. He wore a black pouch slung over his shoulder. Apparently he had something to sell.

The air was rich with spring; sun was warm and yellowed on the asphalt. Mr. Parsons, standing there in front of his hotel and noting the *clack-clack* approach of the sightless man, felt a sudden and foolish sort of pity for all blind creatures.

And, thought Mr. Parsons, he was very glad to be alive. A few years ago he had been little more than a skilled laborer: now he was successful, respected, admired . . . Insurance . . . And he had done it alone, unaided, struggling beneath handicaps . . . And he was still young. The blue air of spring, fresh from its memories of windy pools and lush shrubbery, could thrill him with eagerness.

He took a step forward just as the tap-tapping blind man passed him by. Quickly the shabby fellow turned.

"Listen, guv'nor. Just a minute of your time."

154

Mr. Parsons said, "It's late. I have an appointment. Do you want me to give you something?"

"I ain't no beggar, guv'nor. You bet I ain't. I got a handy little article here"—he pressed a small object into Mr. Parsons' hand—"that I sell. One buck. Best cigarette lighter made."

Mr. Parsons stood there, somewhat annoyed and embarrassed. He was a handsome figure with his immaculate gray suit and gray hat and malacca stick.* Of course the man with the cigarette lighters could not see him ... "But I don't smoke," he said.

———————

*malacca stick: a walking stick, usually made in Asia

"Listen. I bet you know plenty people who smoke. Nice little present," wheedled the man. "And, mister, you wouldn't mind helping a poor guy out?" He clung to Mr. Parsons' sleeve.

Mr. Parsons sighed and felt in his vest pocket. He brought out two half-dollars and pressed them into the man's hand.

"Certainly. I'll help you out. As you say, I can give it to someone. Maybe the elevator boy would—" He hesitated, not wishing to be boorish and inquisitive, even with a blind peddler. "Have you lost your sight entirely?"

The shabby man pocketed the two half-dollars. "Fourteen years, guv'nor." Then he added with an insane sort of pride: "Westbury, sir. I was one of 'em."

"Westbury," repeated Mr. Parsons. "Ah, yes. The chemical explosion . . . The papers haven't mentioned it for years. But at the time it was supposed to be one of the greatest disasters in—"

"They've all forgot about it." The fellow shifted his feet wearily. "I tell you, guv'nor, a man who was in it don't forget about it. Last thing I ever saw was C shop going up in one grand flame, and gas pouring in all the busted windows."

Mr. Parsons coughed. But the blind peddler was caught up with the train of his one dramatic remembrance. And, also, he was thinking that there might be more half-dollars in Mr. Parsons' pocket.

"Just think about it, guv'nor. There was a hundred and eight people killed, about two hundred injured, and over fifty of them lost their eyes. Blind as bats—" He groped forward until his dirty hand rested against Mr. Parsons' coat. "I tell you, sir, there wasn't nothing worse than that in the war. If I had lost my eyes in the war, okay. I would have been well took care of. But I was just a workman, working for what was in it. And I got it. You're right I got it! They was insured, don't worry about that. They—"

"Insured," repeated his listener. "Yes. That's what I sell—"

"You want to know how I lost my eyes?" cried the man. "Well here it is!" His words fell with the bitter and studied drama of a story often told, and told for money. "I was there in C shop, last of all the folks rushing out. Out in the air there was a chance, even with the buildings exploding right and left. A lot of guys made it safe out the door and got away. And just when I was about there, crawling between those big vats, a guy behind me grabs my leg. He says, 'Let me past, you—!' Maybe he was nuts. I dunno. I try to forgive him in my heart, guv'nor. But he was bigger than me. He hauls me back and climbs right over me! Tramples me into the dirt. And he gets out, and I lie there with all that poison gas pouring down on all sides of me, and flame and stuff . . ." He swallowed—a studied sob—and stood dumbly waiting. He could imagine the next words: *Tough luck, my man. Now I want to*—"That's the story, guv'nor."

The spring wind blew past them, damp and quivering.

"Not quite," said Mr. Parsons.

The blind peddler shivered crazily. "Not quite? What do you mean, you—"

"The story is true," Mr. Parsons said, "except that it was the other way around."

"Other way around?" he croaked angrily. "Say, guv'nor—"

"I was in C shop," said Mr. Parsons. "It was the other way around. You were the fellow who hauled me back and climbed over me. You were bigger than I was, Markwardt."

The blind man stood for a long time, swallowing hoarsely. He gulped: "Parsons. I thought you—" And then he screamed fiendishly: "Yes. Maybe so. Maybe so. But I'm blind! I'm blind, and you've been standing here letting me spout to you, and laughing at me every minute! I'm blind."

People in the street turned to stare at him.

"You got away, but I'm blind! Do you hear? I'm—"

Now it's time for YOU to be The Reader as Detective.

What do you think Mr. Parsons answered? Clues in the story should help you answer this question.
Read on to see if you are right!

"Well," said Mr. Parsons, "don't make such a row about it, Markwardt . . . So am I."

I. The Reader as Detective

Read each question below. Then write the letter of the correct answer to each question. Remember, the symbol next to each question identifies the *kind* of reading skill that particular question helps you to develop.

1. The blind beggar lost his eyesight in
   a. the war.
   b. an accident at his house.
   c. a chemical explosion.

2. Mr. Parsons became successful by selling
   a. stocks and bonds.
   b. insurance.
   c. inexpensive cigarette lighters.

3. Following are three sentences from the story. Which sentence is a clue that Mr. Parsons might have been a worker at Westbury?
   a. Mr. Parsons stood there, somewhat annoyed and embarrassed.
   b. A few years ago he had been little more than a skilled laborer.
   c. Mr. Parsons sighed and felt in his vest pocket.

4. At the end of the story, Mr. Parsons told Markwardt not to "make such a row about it." As used in this sentence, the word *row* means
   a. a fuss.   c. a line of things.
   b. to paddle.

5. Which happened first?
   a. The beggar told Mr. Parsons that a bigger man climbed over him in the fire.
   b. Mr. Parsons told the beggar that he was late for an appointment.
   c. Parsons told Markwardt that he, too, was blind.

6. When did the incident at Westbury occur?

   a. last year

   b. four years ago

   c. fourteen years ago

7. Clues in the story suggest that the beggar

   a. told the same story over and over in an effort to gain money.

   b. was really able to see.

   c. knew all along that he was talking to Mr. Parsons.

8. Which one of the following expresses a fact rather than an opinion?

   a. Probably, Mr. Parsons felt sorry for Markwardt later and wrote him a generous check.

   b. The beggar carried a black pouch slung over his shoulder.

   c. All people who are blind feel very sorry for themselves.

9. According to the beggar, how many people were killed?

   a. about fifty

   b. a hundred and eight

   c. two hundred

10. This story is mainly about

   a. a chance meeting between two men who discovered they were involved in an important incident that changed their lives.

   b. how a man saved his life by using his strength.

   c. how many people lost their eyesight in a disaster involving poisonous gas.

II. Looking at Language

As you know, when a word sounds like the thing it describes (*hiss, smash, plop*), this is known as *onomatopoeia*.

The following questions will help you review onomatopoeia when you're looking at language.

11. Find an example of onomatopoeia in the following sentence. The blind beggar was thumping his way before him with the cautious effort of the sightless.

    a. thumping
    b. blind beggar
    c. sightless

12. Below are three expressions found in ''A Man Who Had No Eyes.'' Which one illustrates onomatopoeia?

    a. blind as a bat
    b. poison gas pouring
    c. tap-tapping

13. Identify the sentence from the story which contains an example of onomatopoeia?

    a. ''Other way around?'' he croaked angrily.
    b. The shabby man pocketed the two half-dollars.
    c. You were bigger than I was, Markwardt.

14. Identify an example of onomatopoeia in the following sentence from the story. Mr. Parsons, standing there in front of his hotel and noting the *clack-clack* approach of the sightless man, felt a sudden and foolish sort of pity for all blind creatures.

    a. standing
    b. *clack-clack*
    c. sudden and foolish

15. Following are three groups of words found in the story. Which group illustrates onomatopoeia?

    a. approach, blue, article
    b. gulped, sob, coughed
    c. pride, forgot, windows

III. Finding Word Meanings

Now it's time to be a word detective. Below are ten words which appear in ''A Man Who Had No Eyes.'' Study the words and their definitions. Then complete the following sentences by using each vocabulary word only *once*.

		page
traditional	handed down by custom over the years	154
futile	useless; not successful	154
asphalt	a dark paving material used for surfacing roads	154
handicaps	things that put a person at a disadvantage	154
immaculate	spotless; perfectly clean	155
wheedled	persuaded by coaxing or flattery	156
boorish	rude; having bad manners	156
inquisitive	curious; asking many questions	156
dramatic	full of action; very exciting	156
remembrance	something recalled or kept in mind	156

16. Since Ira is always asking questions and insists on answers, he has a well-deserved reputation for being _____ .

17. Although my grandmother is nearly ninety years old, she has a very clear _____ of her childhood days.

18. Next week, the Department of Parks will begin repairs on the roads in our area; ice has created cracks in the _____ .

19. With flattery and sweet talk, the child _____ his parents into raising his allowance.

20. We will never again invite him to our home; he is impolite, ill-mannered, and _____ .

21. She made a fruitless, or _____ , attempt to catch up to the runner who won the race.

22. I highly recommend the new cleaners; never have my clothes been so _____ .

23. The breathtaking sword duel in the second act was certainly the most _____ scene in the play.

24. One must greatly admire individuals who rise above _____ , or obstacles, to succeed.

25. For as long as I can remember, it has been _____ to hold a Thanksgiving Day parade in our town.

IV. Thinking About the Case

A. We learn that Mr. Parsons had become successful "struggling beneath handicaps," and that he carried a special cane, or "malacca stick." Show how these are clues to Mr. Parsons' final statement.

B. This story is called "A Man Who Had No Eyes." Who is the man referred to in the title of the story? Is it Markwardt or Parsons? Explain your answer.

C. When Markwardt told his story, "his words fell with the bitter and studied drama of a story often told, and told for money." What is the meaning of the words in quotation marks? How successful do you suppose Markwardt was in extracting money through his story? Explain.

The Problem
Solver and the
Spy

by Christopher Anvil

R ichard Verner leaned back in his office chair with
the alert look of a big cat as, across the desk, Nathan Bancroft, a quietly dressed man of average height, spoke
earnestly.

"Last Saturday, a technician at one of our research labo-
ratories got away with the plans for a new and secret type of
laser device. The scientist who invented the device tried to
stop him and was stabbed to death."

Verner nodded intently.

Bancroft went on. "To understand the situation that's
come about, you have to know that the region around this
laboratory has a great many caverns. These are connected in
a gigantic system of natural tunnels, rooms, crevices, and underground streams that have never been thoroughly mapped
or explored.

"The technician who stole the plans is an ardent speleol-
ogist—cave explorer. Possibly one reason for his hobby is that
he suffers from hay fever, and cavern air is pure. In any case,
over a period of years he's spent entire days in an underground series of branching tunnels known as the Maze of Minos. A number of cave explorers have been lost in there, and

163

the local people shun it. The only known expert on this underground maze is the murderer himself.

"Now there's no question, Mr. Verner, but that this spy expected to be far away before the theft of the plans was discovered. But, by sheer good luck, the director of the laboratory discovered what had happened, and immediately notified the police. The police were lucky too—they spotted the technician's car just after the call came in. But then we all ran out of luck. The technician took the plans with him, and escaped into this cavern—this Maze of Minos."

"And got away?" asked Verner.

"Got clean away," said Bancroft. "The tunnels branch off in all directions, and of course it's as dark in there as the blackest possible night. He simply vanished."

Verner nodded again. "He's still in there?"

Bancroft said glumly, "Yes, he's still in there. We have many people on the spot, doing nothing but watching the known exits. But there's always the chance that he'll find some new way out, or knows of one, and will get away. Meanwhile, we desperately need those plans. With the inventor dead, there are certain details we can clear up only from those papers. Yet, if we should get close, he might just take it into his head to destroy them. What we want to do is get to him before he realizes we're near. But how? How do we even *find* him in there?"

"Is he starving?"

"Not likely. He probably has caches of food for his longer explorations. And there's water in the caverns, if you know where to look."

"You want to get him alive, and by surprise?"

"Exactly."

"But he knows you're hunting for him in the cavern?"

"Oh, yes. We've brought in lights, and before we realized what we were up against, we set up loudspeakers and warned him to give up, or we'd come in after him. If he understood what we were saying over all the echoes, this must have amused him immensely. We could put our whole organization in there and get nothing out of a grand-scale search but sore feet, chills, and a dozen people lost in the winding passages. The thing is a standoff, and he knows it."

Verner asked thoughtfully, "And what brings you to me?"

Bancroft smiled. "We've consulted cave explorers, geologists, and all kinds of specialists without finding what we want. Then one of our men remembered General Granger saying that he'd been helped in a difficult case by a 'heuristician.' We got in touch with Granger, who recommended you highly. We didn't know exactly what a 'heuristician' was—but we're prepared to try anything."

Verner laughed. "A heuristician is a professional problem solver. I work on the theory that nearly all problems can be solved by using the same basic technique, combined with ex-

pert knowledge. Some of my cases are scientific, some involve business situations, and others are purely personal problems. The details vary, but the basic technique remains the same. If the case interests me enough to take it, and if the necessary expert help is available, I can usually solve any problem—though sometimes there's an unavoidable element of luck and uncertainty."

"Well," said Bancroft, "we have plenty of experts on hand—all kinds. And I hope that this problem offers enough of a challenge to interest you."

Verner nodded. "We'd better lose no time in getting there."

Many cars and several big trucks were parked outside the main cavern entrance. From outside, electric cables coiled into the brilliantly lighted mouth of the cavern. There was a steady throb of engines as Verner and Bancroft walked in.

Bancroft said, "We're trying to light this end as brightly as possible, and extend the lights inward. But it's a hopeless job. I'll show you why."

They pushed past a small crowd of men, who nodded to Bancroft and glanced at Verner curiously. Then they were in a brightly lighted chamber in the rock. It was about forty feet long by ten high, and twelve to fourteen feet wide. Here their voices and footsteps echoed as Bancroft led the way toward the far end, where a faint breeze of cool air blew in their faces.

"So far, so good," said Bancroft, stepping around a tangle of cables and walking through a narrow doorway cut in the rock. "But here we begin to run into trouble."

He stepped back to show a long brightly lit chamber where fantastic shapes dipped from the ceiling and rose from the floor. Here the electric cables that lay along the floor fanned out in all directions into the well-lighted distance.

Wherever Verner looked, the stalactites and stalagmites rose and dipped endlessly, with new chambers opening out in different directions. As Bancroft led the way, they clambered over the uneven slanting floor past waterfalls of rock, and through little grottoes.

For a long time they walked in silence except for the echoes of their own footsteps. Then suddenly it was dark ahead. The last giant electric bulb lit the shapes of stalagmites rising one behind the other, till the farthest ones were lost in shadows.

A gentle breeze was still in their faces—cool and refreshing, and pure. Somewhere ahead they could hear a faint trickling of water.

"Here," said Bancroft, "we come to the end of our string. These tunnels branch off. Then they open out into rooms, and the rooms have galleries leading off from them, and out of these galleries there are still more tunnels. They twist, wind, and occasionally they even rejoin."

His voice echoed as he talked, and he pointed off to the right. "Over there, somewhere—I think that's the direction—there's an eighty-foot drop with a little stream at the bottom. From the wall of this drop other tunnels open out in various directions and on different levels. There are eyeless fish in the stream, and a kind of blind salamander—very interesting, but our problem is all those tunnels. A man who knew where he was going could pick the one tunnel he wanted out of a dozen or so at any given place. But we have to follow them all. And every so often they divide again or—look up there."

Bancroft pointed to a dark opening above a slope like a frozen waterfall.

"Probably that's another one. This whole place is filled with diverging and connecting tunnels. It's like trying to track down someone inside a man-size termite's nest. We thought he might have left some trace, some sign of where he'd gone. We thought we could follow him with dogs. We forgot that he's practically lived in here during his spare time ever since the laboratory was set up.

"There are plenty of clues. Dogs have followed one track through the dark right over the edge of a sudden drop, and have been killed. We can find signs that he's been just about anywhere we look. We found a pair of sneakers at one place, and food at another." Bancroft shook his head. "Let's go out. There are some people you'll want to meet, now that you've seen what it's like in here, what our problem is."

Outside, in the warm fall night, a group of men quickly gathered around Verner and Bancroft.

One, an old man in dungarees and checked shirt, was well known locally as a cave explorer. A tall man in a gray business suit was the director of the government laboratory, and he repeatedly sneezed and blew his nose. A boy in dungarees and old leather jacket told how he had seen the murderer-spy enter the cave, after crossing a nearby field; he was sure it was the man they were looking for.

"We all knew him. We'd often seen him go in here. He knows more about these caves than anyone—well, except maybe Gramps Peters here."

The old man laughed. "Don't fool yourself. I know old Minotaur, at the other end of this, like I know the back of my hand. But this Maze—I admit I don't know it. I was in here maybe ten years ago, got lost, wandered around for five days, drinking the water in an underground stream, and finally made my way out of a collapsed sinkhole miles away from here. That was the end of the Maze for me. Now, this man you're looking for is a different animal. He's as good as lived in there."

The laboratory director sneezed and blew his nose again. "One reason he spent so much time there, especially in the fall, was the pure air of the caverns. He was, if anything, even more allergic than I am. He once told me that the only place an active man could find recreation out of doors in the fall, if he suffered from hay fever, was inside a cave."

Bancroft said, "We're watching all the known exits. We've sent teams of people through those tunnels, and we've only begun to grasp the difficulties. Somehow, we've *got* to locate him—but how?"

Verner glanced at the old man. "There seems to be a slight, steady current of air in there. That doesn't come from the outside, does it?"

Gramps Peters shook his head. "These passages are complicated, but in this part of the cavern most of the passages slope a little uphill. Up at the other end is what they call the Minotaur. There's an underground riverbed there; no river— but there's this gentle flow of cold air. I suppose the air comes from the outside somewhere, maybe from hundreds of miles away. But you wouldn't know it by the time it gets here. It seems to flow into the Minotaur, and then branch out through the maze. It's always fresh and cool. If you get turned around in a passage, that gentle breeze, when you come to a narrow place, will tell you which way you're headed."

When Verner was finished asking questions, Bancroft took him aside.

"You see now what we're up against, Mr. Verner?"

"I suppose you've got infrared equipment?"

"Yes, and if we knew where he was, it might help us find our way to him in the dark without warning him. But it won't help to send teams out prospecting at random through all those tunnels. The last time we tried it we found nothing, and three people were seriously injured when they came to a sudden slope." He looked at Verner tensely. "Do you have *any* suggestions, any idea at all?"

Verner nodded. "If we're lucky, and if what we've been told is true, we *may* have him out of there in a few hours."

"If you can do that, you're a miracle worker."

"No miracle at all—just common sense. But this is a case

where we'll need a little luck. And we'll have to work from the upper end—from the Minotaur."

The passages of the Minotaur were larger and looked less complicated than those in the Maze. Here the gentle current of cool air seemed stronger, steadier, and could sometimes be felt even in fairly wide passages.

Verner and Bancroft waited tensely. Then down the passage ahead came a small group, carrying a struggling man who was screaming violently.

"*Find* him?" said one of his captors, grinning. "All we had to do was follow the sounds he was making. He was sitting by a cache of food that would have lasted a week, with the plans still in his pocket."

Bancroft was looking at Verner, but he didn't speak. An awful choking and strangling from the prisoner made Bancroft turn in amazement. The choking and strangling noises were mixed with violent sneezing.

Now it's time for YOU to be The Reader as Detective.

How was Verner able to find the spy? Think carefully about the information given in the story. Then decide what Verner did.

Read on to see if you are right!

Down the passage the men had stopped thrashing the stacks of ragweed ordered by Verner. The ragweed had sent thick clouds of pollen drifting through the passage and into the Maze. The pollen had found its target—the murderer-spy who suffered from hay fever.

I. The Reader as Detective

Read each question below. Then write the letter of the correct answer to each question. Remember, the symbol next to each question identifies the *kind* of reading skill that particular question helps you to develop.

1. The spy stole
   a. plans for a kind of laser device.
   b. maps for a gigantic system of underground tunnels.
   c. information about a new and secret type of plane.

2. Which *one* of the following was true of the murderer-spy?
   a. He was almost out of food.
   b. He suffered from hay fever.
   c. He didn't know that he was being hunted.

3. Richard Verner was a "heuristician." A *heuristician* may be defined as
   a. an expert in many languages.
   b. a general, or member of the military.
   c. a professional problem solver.

4. The fact that there was a steady stream of cool air in the tunnels is important because
   a. it kept the hunters cool as they searched for the spy.
   b. it permitted the pollen from the ragweed to be carried to the spy.
   c. it prevented the food in the tunnels from spoiling.

5. Which happened first?
   a. Nathan Bancroft told Richard Verner that the director of the laboratory discovered the crime.
   b. Gramps Peters gave Verner some helpful information.
   c. Verner and Bancroft went to the upper end of the tunnels—the Minotaur.

6. Which one of the following statements expresses an opinion rather than a fact?
   a. Any case can be solved with expert knowledge and luck.
   b. Many people suffer from allergies.
   c. It can sometimes be dangerous to explore long and winding, deep, underground tunnels.

7. Bancroft stated that he was afraid the spy might
  a. commit murder again.
  b. destroy the papers.
  c. get lost in the Maze.

8. Verner explained his "theory" about solving problems. Which expression below best defines the word *theory*?
  a. a charge or fee
  b. happiness or delight
  c. an idea or opinion about something

9. Why did the spy spend so much time in the caverns?
  a. He disliked people and wanted to be alone.
  b. The pure air of the caverns didn't affect his allergy.
  c. He was looking for some plans he had lost there.

10. Suppose this story appeared as a newspaper article. Which of the following would make the best headline?
  a. Ragweed Reveals Criminal in Cave
  b. Spy Seeks Safety in Tricky Tunnels
  c. Scientist Stabbed by Spy on Saturday

II. Looking at Language

As you know, a simile compares two unlike things by using the words *like* or *as*. For example, "He is brave as a lion," is a simile.

A **metaphor**, on the other hand, compares two unlike things without using the words *like* or *as*. For example, "He is a lion," is a metaphor. Another example of a metaphor is, "The stars are a handful of diamonds." Like similes, metaphors help to make language more vivid and descriptive.

11. Identify the sentence which contains a simile.
  a. Richard Verner was extremely alert.
  b. Richard Verner had the alert look of a big cat.
  c. Richard Verner looked like a big cat.

12. Find the sentence which contains a metaphor.

    a. It was unusually dark.
    b. It was dark as night.
    c. The night was a blanket of darkness.

The following sentence contains an unfinished simile. Select the words that best complete the simile.

13. Outside the cavern entrance, the men were

    a. as busy as could be.   *c.* working their heads off.
    b. as busy as bees.

Each sentence in questions 14 and 15 contains an unfinished metaphor. Select the words that best complete the metaphor.

14. Richard Verner was

    a. a walking encyclopedia.
    b. a man who possessed a great deal of knowledge.
    c. as curious as a cat.

15. The complicated cave was

    a. filled with numerous tunnels and passages.
    b. a termite's nest.
    c. like a maze.

15. Select the sentence which contains a metaphor.

    a. The cave had numerous tunnels and passages.
    b. The cave was a termite's nest.
    c. The cave was like a termite's nest.

III. Finding Word Meanings

Now it's time to be a word detective. Below are ten words which appear in "The Problem Solver and the Spy." Study the words and their definitions. Then complete the following sentences by using each vocabulary word only *once.*

		page
intently	earnestly; very seriously	163
ardent	very eager; full of enthusiasm	163
shun	to avoid; keep away from	164
maze	a confusing or puzzling series of winding paths	164
caches	hiding places to store food, supplies, or other things	164
geologists	people who study the earth's crust and its history	165
diverging	branching off; going off in different directions	167
random	by chance; not planned	168
complicated	difficult; hard to solve	169
captors	people who catch or hold a prisoner	169

16. The scientist performed an experiment in which white mice attempted to find their way through a tricky _____ .

17. It is wise to _____ "friends" who continually get into trouble with the law.

18. Stacie runs for an hour five days a week; she is a keen, or _____ , believer in the benefits of jogging.

19. Although this troublesome problem is quite _____ , I believe we are very close to solving it.

20. During the fall, some animals hide food in _____ , so that they will have enough to eat during the long winter months.

21. About a mile ahead you will notice the road _____ ; then you must take the path on the far right-hand side.

22. The _____ brought back samples of rocks which they intended to study.

23. To be accurate, the survey must be of people who have been selected in a completely aimless or _____ manner; so just pick any ten names out of the phone book and call each person.

24. Even though he listened very carefully and _____for fifteen minutes, James still could not understand the point the speaker was making.

25. The kidnap victim stated that his _____had treated him well during the week they held him prisoner.

IV. Thinking About the Case

A. Think about the facts that Richard Verner, the problem solver, learned during the story. Then explain how he used his knowledge to capture the criminal.

B. In Greek legends, the Minotaur was a horrible monster which had the head of a bull and the body of a man. To prevent the Minotaur from escaping, it was imprisoned in a specially built labyrinth (a maze) commissioned by King Minos. Why do you think the author used the terms Maze of Minos and the Minotaur to describe the caverns in the story?

C. Suppose this selection appeared as a television news story. Think of an intriguing opening statement to keep the audience interested.

"A human body," said Dr. Matthews, "is a most difficult thing to get rid of."

The Turn of the Tide

by C. S. Forester

"What always beats them in the end," said Dr. Matthews, "is how to dispose of the body. But, of course, you know that as well as I do."

"Yes," said Slade.

"As a matter of fact," went on Dr. Matthews, warming to the subject to which Slade had so tactfully led him, "it's a terribly knotty problem. It's so difficult, in fact, that I always wonder why anyone is fool enough to commit murder."

"I've often thought the same," Slade said.

"Yes," went on Dr. Matthews, "it's the body that does it, every time. To use poison calls for special facilities, which are good enough to hang you as soon as suspicion is roused. And that suspicion—well, of course, part of my job is to detect poisoning. I don't think anyone can get away with it, nowadays."

"I quite agree with you," said Slade. He had no intention of using poison.

"Well," went on Dr. Matthews, "if you rule out poison, you rule out the chance of getting the body disposed of under the impression that the victim died a natural death. The only other way is to fake things to look like suicide. But you know, and I know, that it just can't be done. You're a lawyer. You've probably read a lot of reports of trials where the murderer has tried it. And you know what's happened to them."

175

"Yes," said Slade.

He certainly had given a great deal of consideration to the matter. It was only after long thought that he had, finally, put aside the notion of disposing of young Spalding and concealing his guilt by a sham* suicide.

"That brings us to where we started, then," said Dr. Matthews. "The only other thing left is to try and conceal the body. And that's more difficult still."

"Yes," said Slade. But he had a perfect plan for disposing of the body.

"A human body," said Dr. Matthews, "is a most difficult thing to get rid of. That chap Oscar Wilde, in that book of his—*Dorian Grey*, isn't it?—gets rid of one by the use of chemicals. Well, I'm a chemist as well as a doctor, and I wouldn't like the job."

"No?" said Slade, politely.

Dr. Matthews was not nearly as clever a man as himself, he thought.

"There's altogether too much of it," said Dr. Matthews. "It's heavy, and it's bulky. Think of all those poor devils who've tried it. Bodies in trunks, and bodies in coal cellars. You can't hide the thing, try as you will."

"Can't I? That's all you know," thought Slade, but aloud he said: "You're quite right. I've never thought about it before."

"Of course, you haven't," agreed Dr. Matthews. "Sensible people don't.

"And yet, you know," he went on, "there's one advantage about getting rid of the body altogether. You're much safer, then. It's a point which ought to interest you, as a lawyer, more than me. It's rather an obscure point of law, but I fancy there are very definite rulings on it. You know what I'm referring to?"

"No, I don't," said Slade, puzzled.

"You can't have a trial for murder unless you can prove there's a victim," said Dr. Matthews. "There's got to be a corpus delicti†, as you lawyers say. A corpse, in other words, even

*sham: fake; false
†corpus delicti (CORE pus di LICK tie): proof of a crime; in this case, the body

if it's only a bit of one. No corpse, no trial. I think that's good law, isn't it?"

"You're right!" said Slade. "I wonder why that hadn't occurred to me before?"

No sooner were the words out of his mouth than he regretted having said them. He was afraid his expression might have hinted at his pleasure in discovering another very reassuring factor in this problem of killing young Spalding. But Dr. Matthews had noticed nothing.

"Well, as I said, the entire destruction of a body is practically impossible. But, I suppose, if a man could achieve it, he would be all right. However strong the suspicion was against him, the police couldn't get him without a corpse. There might be a story in that, Slade, if you or I were writers."

"Yes," assented Slade, and laughed harshly.

There never would be any story about the killing of young Spalding.

"Well," said Dr. Matthews, "we've had a pretty gruesome conversation, haven't we? And I seem to have done all the talking, somehow. That's the result, I suppose, Slade, of the very excellent dinner you gave me. I'd better push off now. Not that the weather is very inviting."

Nor was it. The rain was driving down in a real winter storm, and there was a bitter wind blowing.

"Shouldn't be surprised if this turned to snow before morning," were Dr. Matthew's last words before he drove off.

Slade was glad it was such a tempestuous night. It meant that, more certainly than ever, there would be no one out in the lanes, no one out on the sands when he disposed of young Spalding's body.

Back in his room, Slade looked at the clock. There was still an hour to spare; he could spend it in making sure that his plans were all correct.

He looked up the tide tables. Yes, that was right. Spring tides. The lowest of low water on the sands. There was not so much luck about that; young Spalding came back on the midnight train every Wednesday night, and it was not surprising that, sooner or later, the Wednesday night would coincide with a spring tide. But it was lucky that this particular

Wednesday night should be one of tempest; luckier still that low water should be at one-thirty, the best time for him.

He opened the door and listened carefully. He could not hear a sound. Mrs. Dumbleton, his housekeeper, must have been in bed some time now and would not hear his departure. Nor his return, when Spalding had been killed and disposed of.

The hands of the clock seemed to be moving very fast. He must make sure everything was correct. The chain and the other iron weights were already in the back seat of the car; he had put them there before old Matthews arrived to dine. He slipped on his overcoat.

From his desk, Slade took a curious little bit of apparatus: eighteen inches of strong cord, tied at each end to a six-inch length of wood so as to make a ring. He made a last close examination to see that the knots were quite firm, and then he put it in his pocket; as he did so, he ran through, in his mind, the words—he knew them by heart—of the passage in the book about the Thugs of India, describing the method of strangulation* employed by them.

He could think quite coldly about all this. Young Spalding was a busybody. A word from him, now, could bring ruin upon Slade, could send him to prison.

Slade thought of other defaulting solicitors† he had heard of. He remembered remarks about them. He thought of having to beg his bread in the streets on his release from prison, of cold and misery and starvation. Never, never, would he endure it.

What right had young Spalding to condemn a gray-haired man twenty years his senior to such a fate? If nothing but death would stop him, then he deserved to die. He clenched his hand on the cord in his pocket.

A glance at the clock told him he had better be moving. He turned out the lights and tiptoed out of the house, shutting the door quietly. The bitter wind flung icy rain into his face, but he did not notice it. He pushed the car out of the garage by hand and locked the garage doors, as a precaution against the chance that someone should notice that his car was out.

---

*strangulation: choking
†defaulting solicitors: lawyers who fail to pay money they are in charge of

He drove cautiously down the road. Of course, there was not a soul about in a quiet place like this. The few street lamps were already extinguished.

There were lights in the station as he drove over the bridge; they were awaiting there the arrival of the twelve-thirty train. Spalding would be on that. Every Wednesday he went to his subsidiary office*, sixty miles away. Slade turned into the lane a quarter of a mile beyond the station and then reversed his car so that it pointed toward the road. He put out the side lights, and settled himself to wait; his hand fumbled with the cord in his pocket.

The train was a little late. Slade had been waiting a quarter of an hour when he saw the lights of the train come to a standstill in the station. Then the train moved slowly out again. As soon as it was gone, the lights in the station began to go out, one by one.

Next, Slade's straining ears heard footsteps.

Young Spalding was striding down the road. With his head bent before the storm, he did not notice the motor car in the lane, and he walked past it.

Slade counted up to two hundred, slowly, and then he switched on his lights, started the engine, and drove the car out into the road in pursuit. He saw Spalding and drew up alongside.

"Is that Spalding?" he said, striving to make the tone of his voice as natural as possible. "I'd better give you a lift, hadn't I?"

"Thanks very much," said Spalding. "This isn't the sort of night to walk two miles in."

He climbed in and shut the door. No one had seen. No one would know. Slade drove slowly down the road.

"Bit of luck, seeing you," he said. "I was just on my way home from bridge at Mrs. Clay's when I saw the train come in and remembered it was Wednesday and you'd be walking home. So I thought I'd turn a bit out of my way to take you along."

"Very good of you, I'm sure," said Spalding.

"As a matter of fact," said Slade, speaking slowly and driving slowly, "I wanted to talk business to you, as it happened."

---

*subsidiary office: a branch office; an office which is part of a larger company

"Rather an odd time to talk business," said Spalding. "Can't it wait till tomorrow?"

"No, it cannot," said Slade. "It's about the Vere trust."

"Oh, yes. I wrote to remind you last week that you had to make delivery*."

"Yes, you did. And I told you, long before that, that it would be inconvenient, with Hammond abroad."

"I don't see that," said Spalding. "I don't see that Hammond's got anything to do with it."

"As I said, it would be inconvenient."

Slade brought the car to a standstill at the side of the road.

"Look here, Spalding," he said, desperately, "I've never asked a favor of you before. But now I ask you, as a favor, to forgo† delivery for a bit. Just for three months, Spalding."

But Slade had small hope that his request would be granted. So little hope, in fact, that he brought his left hand out of his pocket holding the piece of wood, with the loop of cord dangling from its ends. He put his arm around the back of Spalding's seat.

"No, I can't, really I can't," said Spalding. "I've got my duty to my clients to consider. I'm sorry to insist, but you're quite well aware of what my duty is."

"Yes," said Slade. "But I beg you to wait."

"I see," said Spalding, after a long pause.

"I only want three months," pressed Slade. "Just three months."

Spalding hardened his heart. "No," he said. "I can't promise anything like that. I don't think it's any use continuing this discussion. Perhaps I'd better walk home from here."

He put out his hand to the latch of the door, and, as he did so, Slade jerked the loop of cord over his head. A single turn of Slade's wrist tightened the cord about Spalding's throat. Spalding never drew breath at all. He lost consciousness long before he was dead.

Nobody had seen, nobody would know.

Slade had gained, now, the time in which he could get his affairs into order. It only remained to dispose of Spalding's body, and he had planned to do that very satisfactorily. Just for a moment Slade felt as if all this were only some dream,

---

*make delivery: make a payment of money
†forgo: put off; do without

some nightmare, but then he came back to reality and went on with the plan he had in mind.

He pulled the dead man's knees forward so that the corpse lay back in the seat. He put the car in gear, and drove rapidly down the road—much faster than when he had been arguing with Spalding. Low water was in three-quarters of an hour's time, and the sands were ten miles away.

Slade drove fast through the wild night. There was not a soul about in those lonely lanes. He knew the way by heart— he had driven repeatedly over that route recently in order to memorize it.

The car bumped down the last bit of lane, and Slade drew up on the edge of the sands.

It was pitch dark, and the bitter wind was howling about him, under the black sky. Despite the noise of the wind, he could hear the surf breaking far away, two miles away, across the level sands. He climbed out of the driver's seat and walked round to the other door. When he opened it the dead man fell sideways, into his arms.

With an effort, Slade held him up, while he groped into the back of the car for the chain and the iron weights. He crammed the weights into the dead man's pockets, and he wound the chain round and round the dead man's body, tucking in the ends to make it all secure. With that mass of iron to hold it down, the body would never be found again when dropped into the sea at the lowest ebb of spring tide.

Slade tried now to lift the body in his arms, to carry it over the sands. He reeled and strained, but he was not strong enough—Slade was a man of slight figure, and past his prime. The sweat on his forehead was icy in the icy wind.

For a second, doubt overwhelmed him, lest all his plans should fail for want of bodily strength. But he forced himself into thinking clearly; he forced his frail body into obeying the commands of his brain.

He turned round, still holding the dead man upright. Stooping, he got the heavy burden on his shoulders. He drew the arms round his neck and, with effort, he got the legs up round his hips. The dead man now rode him pick-a-back.* Bending nearly double, he was able to carry the heavy weight

---

*pick-a-back: piggyback—on the back; in this case, carried over the back and shoulders

in this fashion, the arms tight round his neck, the legs tight round his waist.

He set off, staggering, down the slope of the sands toward the sound of the surf. The sands were soft beneath his feet—it was because of this softness that he had not driven the car down to the water's edge. He could afford to take no chances.

The icy wind shrieked round him all that long way. The tide was nearly two miles out. That was why Slade had chosen this place. In the depth of winter, no one would go out to the water's edge at low tide for months.

He staggered on over the sands, clasping the limbs of the body close about him. Desperately, he forced himself forward, not stopping to rest, for he only just had time now to reach the water's edge before the flow began. He went on and on, driving his exhausted body with fierce urgings from his frightened brain.

Then, at last, he saw it: a line of white in the darkness which indicated the water's edge. Farther out, the waves were breaking.

He was going to make quite sure of things. Steadying himself, he stepped into the water, wading in farther and farther so as to be able to drop the body into comparatively deep water. He held to his resolve, staggering through the icy water, knee deep, thigh deep, until it was nearly at his waist. This was far enough. He stopped, gasping in the darkness.

He leaned over to one side, to roll the body off his back. It did not move. He pulled at its arms. They were obstinate. He could not loosen them. He shook himself, wildly. He tore at the legs round his waist. Still the thing clung to him. Wild with panic and fear, he flung himself about in a mad effort to rid himself of the burden. It clung on as though it were alive. He could not break its grip.

Then another breaker* came in. It splashed about him, wetting him far above his waist. The tide had begun to turn now, and the tide on those sands comes in like a racehorse.

He made another effort to cast off the load, and when it still held him fast, he lost his nerve and tried to struggle out of the sea. But it was too much for his exhausted body. The weight of the corpse and of the iron with which it was loaded overbore him. He fell.

He struggled up again in the foam-streaked, dark sea, staggered a few steps, fell again—and did not rise. The dead man's arms were round his neck, strangling him.

> Now it's time for YOU to be The Reader as Detective.
>
> Why couldn't Slade free himself from Spalding's arms which were strangling him?
> Read on to see if you are right!

Rigor mortis† had set in and Spalding's muscles had refused to relax.

---

*breaker: wave
†rigor mortis: the stiffening of the body that takes place after death

I. The Reader as Detective

Read each question below. Then write the letter of the correct answer to each question. Remember, the symbol next to each question identifies the *kind* of reading skill that particular question helps you to develop.

1. Slade was afraid that Spalding

    a. would fire him.

    b. would refuse to lend him money.

    c. would have him sent to prison.

2. Slade planned to get rid of Spalding's body by

    a. burying it in deep sand.

    b. weighing it down in the sea.

    c. using chemicals.

3. Clues in the story suggest that Slade thought he would get away with the crime because

    a. Spalding's body would never be found.

    b. he could prove he was home when the crime was committed.

    c. Dr. Matthews would say that Slade was with him when Spalding was murdered.

4. According to Dr. Matthews, all the talk about murder had led to "a pretty gruesome conversation." What is the meaning of the word *gruesome*?

    a. charming

    b. horrible

    c. enjoyable

5. Which happened last?

    a. Slade and Dr. Matthews had an excellent dinner together.

    b. Slade tried to carry the body toward the water.

    c. Spalding refused to grant Slade an additional three months.

6. Slade thought that Spalding had no right "to condemn a gray-haired man twenty years his senior." From this statement, we may infer that

   a. Slade and Spalding were both about twenty years old.
   b. Slade was twenty years older than Spalding.
   c. Slade was twenty years younger than Spalding.

7. Which *one* of the following statements expresses a fact rather than an opinion?

   a. In view of the situation he was in, Slade was right to try to get rid of Spalding.
   b. If Slade had succeeded with his plan, he definitely would have gotten away with the crime.
   c. Slade attempted his crime on a night that was bitterly cold and stormy.

8. What probably happened to Slade?

   a. He was eventually drowned by the tide.
   b. He was caught and sent to jail.
   c. He freed himself and swam to safety.

9. According to the author, "Slade was a man of slight figure and past his prime." Which expression best defines the word *prime* as used in this sentence?

   a. best condition
   b. a number in mathematics
   c. chief or boss

10. This story tells mostly about

   a. how a doctor and a lawyer discussed why anyone would be a fool to commit murder.
   b. how a man planned and executed a murder, and then was "killed" by his victim.
   c. how one lawyer asked another to do him a favor.

II. Looking at Language

As you know, powerful adjectives, vivid verbs, similes and metaphors all help to make writing more colorful and descriptive. Alliteration (the repetition of consonant sounds) often lends rhythm and a musical quality.

The following questions will help you review these elements as you're looking at language.

11. Which one of the following sentences illustrates alliteration?

a. He deserved to die a dismal death.
b. Every Wednesday, he traveled to his office sixty miles away.
c. His hand fumbled with the cord in his pocket.

12. Identify the vivid verbs in the following sentence. The icy wind shrieked round him as he reeled desperately toward the water.

a. icy, desperately
b. shrieked, reeled
c. wind, water

13. Following are three statements found in the story. Which one contains a simile?

a. Wild with panic and fear, he flung himself about in a mad effort.
b. There was not a soul about in those lonely lanes.
c. The tide on those sands comes in like a racehorse.

14. Slade "went on and on, dragging his exhausted body with fierce urgings from his frightened brain." The words *exhausted, fierce,* and *frightened* are

a. vivid verbs.
b. powerful adjectives.
c. metaphors.

15. Following are three sentences from the story. Which one best illustrates alliteration?

a. For a second, doubt overwhelmed him, lest all his plans should fail for want of bodily strength.
b. He set off, staggering, down the slope of the sands toward the sound of the surf.
c. The hands of the clock seemed to be moving very fast.

III. Finding Word Meanings

Now it's time to be a word detective. Below are ten words which appear in "The Turn of the Tide." Study the words and their definitions. Then complete the following sentences by using each vocabulary word only *once*.

		page
tactfully	in a thoughtful, skillful, and considerate way	175
obscure	not clear; hard to understand	176
tempestuous	stormy; violent	177
coincide	to be exactly alike; to occur at the same time	177
apparatus	tools, machines, or other equipment	178
precautions	care taken in advance to protect against bad results	178
extinguished	wiped out	179
inconvenient	troublesome; causing difficulty or bother	180
crammed	stuffed; forced into	181
comparatively	relatively; in a similar way	183

16. Because of the _____weather, trees were overturned, power lines were blown down, and telephone power was interrupted.

17. Since our lunch periods _____ , Pat and I always have lunch together at 12:30.

18. The top drawer of my desk is so _____with odds and ends, it is difficult to open it.

19. When our three best players were injured, our chances of finishing first were just about _____ .

20. If it is not too _____for you, would you mind dropping me off at the library after work?

21. Saws, drills, and electric sanders are some of the _____ used by carpenters.

22. The point of your essay is vague; perhaps you should write your composition over to make it less _____ .

23. When we leave our house to go on vacation, we always stop the mail and leave some lights on; these are some _____ we take against crime.

24. Since the weather is usually around forty degrees this time of year, today's 55-degree temperature is _____ warm.

25. Unfortunately, we have some bad news for Mildred; someone must speak to her gently and _____ .

IV. Thinking About the Case

A. "The Turn of the Tide" is an excellent title for this selection. Think about what happened. Then discuss the different ways in which the tide turned in this story.

B. The author states that because of the softness of the sand, Slade "had not driven the car down to the water's edge. He could afford to take no chances." What chances would Slade have taken had he driven down to the water?

C. Suppose that Slade succeeded in disposing of Spalding's body. Find clues in the story which would make the police suspicious of Slade.

"How can I get the idea across to you that every word I have submitted was actually written by me! I have never copied any material from Todd Thromberry, nor have I ever seen any of his writings."

Who's Cribbing?

by Jack Lewis

April 2, 1952

Mr. Jack Lewis
90-26 219 St.
Queens Village, N.Y.

Dear Mr. Lewis:

We are returning your manuscript "The Ninth Dimension." At first glance, I had figured it a story well worthy of publication. Why wouldn't I? So did the editors of *Cosmic Tales* back in 1934 when the story was first published.

As you no doubt know, it was the great Todd Thromberry who wrote the story you tried to pass off on us as an original. Let me give you a word of caution concerning the penalties resulting from plagiarism*.

It's not worth it. Believe me.

Sincerely,
Doyle P. Gates
Science Fiction Editor
Deep Space Magazine

---

*plagiarism: using another writer's work and passing it off as your own

189

April 5, 1952

Mr. Doyle P. Gates, Editor
Deep Space Magazine
New York, N.Y.

Dear Mr. Gates:

I do not know, nor am I aware of the existence of any Todd Thromberry. The story you rejected was submitted in good faith, and I resent the inference that I plagiarized it.

"The Ninth Dimension" was written by me not more than a month ago, and if there is any similarity between it and the story written by this Thromberry person, it is purely coincidental.

However, it has set me thinking. Some time ago, I submitted another story to *Stardust Scientifiction* and received a penciled notation on the rejection slip stating that the story was, "too thromberryish."

Who is Todd Thromberry? I don't remember reading anything written by him in the ten years I've been interested in science fiction.

Sincerely,
Jack Lewis

April 11, 1952

Mr. Jack Lewis
90-26 219 St.
Queens Village, N.Y.

Dear Mr. Lewis:

Re: Your letter of April 5.

While the editors of this magazine are not in the habit of making open accusations and are well aware of the fact in the writing business there will always be some overlapping of plot ideas, it is very hard for us to believe that you are not familiar with the works of Todd Thromberry.

While Mr. Thromberry is no longer among us, his works, like so many other writers', only became widely recognized after his death in 1941. Perhaps it was his work in the field of electronics that supplied him with the bottomless pit of new ideas so apparent in all his works. Nevertheless, even at this stage of science fiction's development it is apparent that he had a style that many of our so-called contemporary writers might do well to copy. By "copy," I do not mean rewrite word for word one or more of his works, as you have done. For while you state this has been accidental, surely you must realize that the chance of this phenomenon actually happening is about a million times as great as the occurrence of four pat royal flushes on one deal.

Sorry, but we're not that naive.

Sincerely yours,
Doyle P. Gates
Science Fiction Editor
Deep Space Magazine

April 14, 1952

Mr. Doyle P. Gates, Editor
Deep Space Magazine
New York, N.Y.

Sir:

Your accusations are typical of the rag you publish. Please cancel my subscription immediately.

Sincerely,
Jack Lewis

April 14, 1952

Science Fiction Society
144 Front Street
Chicago, Ill.

Gentlemen:

I am interested in reading some of the works of the late Todd Thromberry.

I would like to get some of the publications that feature his stories.

Respectfully,
Jack Lewis

April 22, 1952

Mr. Jack Lewis
90-26 219 St.
Queens Village, N.Y.

Dear Mr. Lewis:

So would we. All I can suggest is that you contact the publishers if any are still in business, or haunt your second-hand bookstores.

If you succeed in getting any of these magazines, please let us know. We'll pay you a handsome premium on them.

> Yours,
> Ray Albert
> President
> Science Fiction Society

May 11, 1952

Mr. Sampson J. Gross, Editor
Strange Worlds Magazine
St. Louis, Mo.

Dear Mr. Gross:

I am enclosing the manuscript of a story I have just completed. As you see on the title page, I call it "Wreckers of Ten Million Galaxies." Because of the great amount of research that went into it, I must set the minimum price on this one at not less than two cents a word.

Hoping you will see fit to use it for publication in your magazine, I remain,

> Respectfully,
> Jack Lewis

May 19, 1952

Mr. Jack Lewis
90-26 219 St.
Queens Village, N.Y.

Dear Mr. Lewis:

I'm sorry, but at the present time we won't be able to use "Wreckers of Ten Million Galaxies." It's a great yarn though, and if at some future date we decide to use it we will make

out the reprint check directly to the estate of Todd Thromberry.

That boy sure could write.

> Cordially,
> Sampson J. Gross
> Editor
> *Strange Worlds Magazine*

May 23, 1952

Mr. Doyle P. Gates, Editor
Deep Space Magazine
New York, N.Y.

Dear Mr. Gates:

While I said I would never have any dealings with you or
your magazine again, a situation has arisen which is most
puzzling.

It seems all my stories are being returned to me by reason
of the fact that except for the byline, they are exact duplicates
of the works of this Todd Thromberry person.

In your last letter you aptly described the odds on the accidental occurrence of this phenomenon in the case of one
story. What would you consider the approximate odds on no
less than half a dozen of my writings?

I agree with you—astronomical!

Yet in the interest of all humanity, how can I get the idea
across to you that every word I have submitted was actually
written *by me*! I have never copied any material from Todd
Thromberry, nor have I ever seen any of his writings. In fact,
as I told you in one of my letters, up until a short while ago
I was totally unaware of his very existence.

An idea has occurred to me however. It's a truly weird
theory, and one that I probably wouldn't even suggest to anyone but a science fiction editor. But suppose—just suppose—
that this Thromberry person, what with his experiments in
electronics and everything, had in some way managed to
crack through this time-space barrier mentioned so often in
your magazine. And suppose—egotistical as it sounds—he had

singled out my work as being the type of material he had always wanted to write.

Do you begin to follow me? Or is the idea of a person from a different time cycle looking over my shoulder while I write too fantastic for you to accept?

Please write and tell me what you think of my theory?

Respectfully,
Jack Lewis

May 25, 1952

Mr. Jack Lewis
90-26 219 St.
Queens Village, N.Y.

Dear Mr. Lewis:

We think you should consult a psychiatrist.

Sincerely,
Doyle P. Gates
Science Fiction Editor
Deep Space Magazine

June 3, 1952

Mr. Sam Mines
Science Fiction-Editor
Standard Magazines Inc.
New York, N.Y.

Dear Mr. Mines:

While the enclosed is not really a manuscript at all, I am submitting this series of letters, carbon copies, and correspondence, in the hope that you might give some credulity* to this seemingly unbelievable happening.

The enclosed letters are all in proper order and should be self-explanatory. Perhaps if you publish them, some of your

---

*credulity: believability

readers might have some idea how this phenomenon could be explained.

I call the entire piece "Who's Cribbing*?"

Respectfully,
Jack Lewis

> Now it's time for YOU to be The Reader as Detective.
>
> What do you think Mr. Mines wrote in the letter he sent to Jack Lewis? If you have been actively involved as The Reader as Detective as you read this book, you should have a pretty good idea.
>
> Now read on to see if you are right!

June 10, 1952

Mr. Jack Lewis
90-26 219 St.
Queens Village, N.Y.

Dear Mr. Lewis:

Your idea of a series of letters to put across a science-fiction idea is an intriguing one, but I'm afraid it doesn't quite come off.

It was in the August 1940 issue of *Macabre Adventures* that Mr. Thromberry first used this very idea. Ironically enough, the story title also was "Who's Cribbing?"

Feel free to contact us again when you have something more original.

Yours,
Samuel Mines
Science Fiction Editor
Standard Magazines Inc.

---

*cribbing: passing off another person's writing as one's own

I. The Reader as Detective

Read each question below. Then write the letter of the correct answer to each question. Remember, the symbol next to each question identifies the *kind* of reading skill that particular question helps you to develop.

1. All of Jack Lewis' stories were sent back to him because
   a. they were not very interesting.
   b. they had already been written by Todd Thromberry.
   c. he would not accept less than two cents a word for them.

2. What kind of works did Jack Lewis write?
   a. science-fiction stories
   b. true-to-life accounts of living people
   c. humorous books for young children

3. Evidence in the story suggests that Mr. Gates thought that Jack Lewis
   a. had mental problems.
   b. was an excellent writer.
   c. was really Todd Thromberry.

4. The odds against two authors writing exactly the same story are described as "astronomical." What is the meaning of the word *astronomical*?
   a. slight   b. possible   c. enormous

5. Which happened last?
   a. Lewis sent his manuscript, "The Ninth Dimension," to a magazine.
   b. Mr. Mines wrote Lewis that using a series of letters to make a point was an idea that had been used before.
   c. Lewis attempted to find some stories written by Thromberry.

6. Judging by the dates in the letters, we may infer that this story was written
   a. very recently.
   b. about ten years ago.
   c. more than forty years ago.

7. Which one of the following statements expresses an opinion rather than a fact?

    a. Thromberry was probably communicating to Lewis from outer space.

    b. It was difficult to find copies of magazines that had stories by Thromberry.

    c. Thromberry died in 1941.

8. The stories of Lewis and Thromberry were "duplicates." What is the meaning of the word *duplicates*?

    a. very funny

    b. quite short

    c. exact copies

9. When Lewis received the final letter in the story, he probably felt

    a. pleased.

    b. amused.

    c. shocked.

10. Which of the following would make the best headline for this story?

    a. Magazines Refuse to Print Writer's Works

    b. Writer's Works Already Written by Another Writer

    c. Writer Jailed for Stealing Other Writer's Works

II. Looking at Language

You know that it is often possible to figure out the meaning of a difficult or unfamiliar word by looking at the *context*—the words (and sometimes the sentences)—around the word. The following questions will give you additional practice in using context clues to find a word's meaning.

11. All of Lewis' stories were returned to him and were rejected for the same reason. What is the meaning of the word *rejected*?

    a. purchased

    b. turned down

    c. printed again

12. Ray Albert wrote Lewis: "If you succeed in getting any of these magazines, please let us know. We'll pay you a handsome premium on them." Use context clues to decide which expression best defines the word *premium.*

    a. an unusually high price
    b. money for an insurance policy
    c. a small sum of cash

13. Lewis wrote Mr. Gates: "Is the idea of a person from a different time cycle looking over my shoulder while I write too fantastic for you to accept?" What is the meaning of the word *fantastic* as used in this sentence?

    a. great or wonderful
    b. strange or weird
    c. boring or dull

14. An angry Lewis wrote *Deep Space Magazine* and stated that their charges "are typical of the rag you publish. Please cancel my subscription immediately." What is the meaning of the word *cancel?*

    a. reduce
    b. punch
    c. stop

15. Refer to the question above. Then select the answer which best defines the word *subscription.*

    a. the right to receive a magazine by paying a sum of money
    b. stories sent to a magazine
    c. a letter to the editor

III. Finding Word Meanings

Now it's time to be a word detective. Following are ten words which appear in "Who's Cribbing?" Study the words and their definitions. Then complete the following sentences by using each vocabulary word only *once.*

		page
notation	a note or remark	190
accusation	a charge of having done something wrong	190
contemporary	of the present time; current; modern	191
phenomenon	something striking, unusual, rare, or remarkable	191
naive	easily fooled or deceived; accepting things without considering them carefully	191
publications	newspapers, books, or magazines; things that are published	192
aptly	appropriately; suitably	194
egotistical	boastful and conceited; overly concerned with one's self	194
correspondence	the exchange of letters; communication by letters	195
intriguing	arousing interest	196

16. The clerk was charged with theft, but the _____ eventually proved false.

17. Every seventy-six years, Halley's comet can be seen in the sky; it is a rare and unusual _____ .

18. On the margin of the letter was a(n) _____ that said, "Please see me about this tomorrow."

19. It is not possible to have a meaningful conversation with him because he is so conceited and _____ , he talks of nothing but himself.

20. Over the years they had a long _____ ; after they were married, they enjoyed reading the letters they had written to each other.

21. The anthology contained works by ancient writers, as well as some selections by current, or _____ authors.

22. It is easy to take advantage of people who are _____ because they are so easily misled and made victims.

23. The first few pages of the book were so _____ , I found that I could not put the book down.

24. Her recent discoveries about undersea life have been printed in many of the leading scientific _____ .

25. Since Thomas Edison created more than 1,100 inventions and also lived in Menlo Park, New Jersey, he is _____called "The Wizard of Menlo Park."

IV. Thinking About the Case

A. Here's a chance to use your imagination. Think about the story. Then make up a reasonable explanation of why Lewis kept writing Thromberry's stories.

B. Suppose that Lewis answered the last letter in the story. What do you think he would have written?

C. Why is this story called "Who's Cribbing?"? Think of another interesting, appropriate title.

GLOSSARY

A

accumulation a collection of
accusation a charge of having done something wrong
administer to manage or supervise
aide helper; assistant
ajar slightly open
alias a false or assumed name
allergic having a strong bodily response or reaction, such as coughing or sneezing, to certain pollens, foods, etc.
aloof not involved
anonymous having an unknown name
apparatus tools, machines, or other equipment
apparent obvious; plain to see or understand
aptly appropriately; suitably
ardent very eager; full of enthusiasm
arrogant too proud or self-important
arsenic a powerful poison
aspect a particular part
asphalt a dark paving material used for surfacing roads
assented agreed; consented
associated connected with or joined
attentive paying attention
audit an examination of records or accounts

B

balk to stop short and refuse to continue
behest order or command
belligerent at war or warlike; in a very unfriendly and angry manner
benefactors people who give money or help to others
bizarre extremely odd or strange
boorish rude; having bad manners
brawl a noisy quarrel or fight; to quarrel or fight
brazen bold; having no shame

C

caches hiding places to store food, supplies, or other things

captors   people who catch or hold a prisoner
catastrophe   a terrible disaster
coaxed   persuaded or influenced by using a gentle manner
coincide   to be exactly alike; to occur at the same time
coincidental   happening by chance
comparatively   relatively; in a similar way
compelled   required; forced or commanded
complicated   difficult; hard to solve
concise   brief but full of meaning
consoled   comforted; eased the grief of
contemporary   of the present time; current; modern
contempt   held in low regards; scorned
contends   declares to be true
correspondence   the exchange of letters; communication by letters
countenance   appearance, especially the expression of the face
counterfeit   false; not genuine, usually intended to deceive
crammed   stuffed; forced into
cremation   the burning to ashes of a dead body
crepe paper   a thin, rippled paper used for decorations
cringe   to draw back with fear

D

dauntless   bold; fearless
debris   scattered ruins or remains
deceitful   deceiving; lying
decomposed   rotten; broken apart
deduce   figure out by reasoning
destination   the place where someone or something is headed
destiny   what finally becomes of a person or thing; one's fate
detached   separate, not influenced by others
devoid   entirely without, lacking
dictated   required; ordered
dilute   to weaken; make thinner
diminish   to make smaller; decrease
disbelief   lack of belief
disclosed   made known; told
discolored   change or spoiled the color of
discontent   unhappy; not satisfied
disgruntled   unhappy; not content
disregarding   ignoring; paying no attention to
dissatisfied   not satisfied
diverging   branching off; going off in different directions
doff   to remove; take off
dour   gloomy or sullen

drab dull
dramatic full of action; very exciting
dredge to dig up
drivel silly talk; nonsense
duly in a proper way or manner
duration length of time

E

ebb the flowing of the tide away from the shore
egotistical boastful and conceited; overly concerned with one's self
elated filled with joy
elevates raises
elude to escape from; avoid
emphasize to stress or give special force to
endeavored attempted strongly; tried hard
enrich to make more valuable
entanglement a very tricky, confusing, or complicated situation
entitled having a legal right or claim to something
entrust to give over to another for protection or care
err to make a mistake; go wrong
evade escape; avoid
excel to be better than; to be superior at
exceptionally unusually; to an extraordinary degree
extinguished wiped out
extracted drew out

F

fanatic someone who is carried away or moved beyond reason because of feelings or beliefs
flaw a slight error or mistake
flinch to draw back suddenly with pain or surprise
foible a small fault or weak point
fragile easily broken
frail weak
fugitive one who flees or runs away, especially from the law or justice
futile useless; not successful

G

galled annoyed; irritated
genial friendly; pleasant
geologists people who study the earth's crust and its history

grooming   taking care of the appearance of; brushing
guarantee   a pledge or promise that something will be done
gutted   removed the insides of

H

handicaps   things that put a person at a disadvantage
hilarious   unusually funny or humorous
hoarder   a person who gathers and stores money, food, supplies, etc.

I

immaculate   spotless; perfectly clean
incapable   not able to
inconvenient   troublesome; causing difficulty or bother
indebted   obligated; owing
inference   conclusion
infrared   certain invisible but powerful rays of light
ingenious   brilliant; unusually clever
inherited   received from an ancestor
inquisitive   curious; asking many questions
insight   the ability to recognize, or see into the true nature of something
insure   to make sure of or certain; to protect
intact   untouched; whole or complete
intently   earnestly; very seriously
intriguing   arousing interest
irk   bothers; annoys
irritated   annoyed; bothered
itemize   to list unit by unit

J

jostling   pushing; shoving
jovial   full of fun; very merry

K

kindling   small pieces of wood for starting a fire

L

laser   a device that produces a very narrow and powerful beam of light
latching   holding onto
legible   able to be read easily

logical   reasonable; of good sense and reason
lush   growing abundantly, thick and green

M

manuscript   a typewritten or handwritten copy of a book, article, or story
mason   a person who works with brick or stone
maze   a confusing or puzzling series of winding paths
meager   thin or lean; slight
mistrusted   doubted; failed to believe
morphia   a drug which causes sleepiness, used to dull pain
mortar   a mixture of cement, sand, lime, and water used for holding stones or bricks together
multicolored   having many colors

N

naive   easily fooled or deceived; accepting things without considering them carefully
narrative   a story or description of events, real or imaginary
nominal   in name only; slight; not meaningful
notation   a note or remark
novelty   something fresh or unusual; newness
numeral   a figure or word that stands for a number

O

obscure   not clear; hard to understand
obstinate   stubborn

P

parched   thirsty; dry
pathetic   arousing pity and sympathy
phenomenon   something striking; unusual, rare, or remarkable
plausible   reasonable; likely
podium   a raised platform for a speaker or performer
precautions   care taken in advance to protect against bad results
precisely   exactly
proposition   a plan or idea offered for acceptance
proprietor   owner
prosperous   successful; doing well
protruding   pushing or thrusting outward
provisions   a supply of food or drink
provoked   moved to action; bothered

psychiatrist   a doctor who studies and/or treats mental problems
publications   newspapers, books, or magazines; things that are published

Q

quest   a search; hunt
quizzically   in a questioning way; puzzlingly

R

radiance   vivid brightness
random   by chance; not planned
reaction   response
recoiled   jumped or sprang back
recommendation   a suggestion
regularity   in a usual or regular manner
reinforce   to strengthen
reliance   trust; confidence
reluctance   resistance; unwillingness
remembrance   something recalled or kept in mind
remit   to send money
reputable   well thought of; honorable
respective   belonging to each; particular
responded   answered; replied
retained   kept; held

S

salamander   a lizard-shaped animal which lives in water and damp places
salutation   a word or phrase of greeting
sane   of sound mind
scoundrel   wicked person; rascal
scrawl   careless or poor handwriting
securities   stocks, bonds, or other valuable certificates
self-explanatory   obvious; needing no explanation
sequence   a connected series or order
shun   to avoid; keep away from
similarity   likeness; resemblance
sinister   evil; threatening
skinflint   a miser or stingy person
slinked   moved in a guilty or sneaking manner
slung   thrown
smug   too pleased with one's self

specialists   people who study, pursue, or are expert in, a particular field

spendthrift   a person who is wasteful with money

squandered   spent foolishly; wasted

stalactite   an icicle-like formation of lime which hangs from the roof of a cave

stalagmite   a cone-like formation of lime built up on the floor of a cave

stamina   endurance; strength

streamers   long, narrow strips of paper or cloth for decorations

subtle   not obvious; very clever

suede   a soft leather; or leather-like fabric

sulking   gloomy and bad tempered

surgeon   a doctor who performs operations

T

tactfully   in a thoughtful, skillful, and considerate way

technique   a particular method; technical skill

tempestuous   stormy; violent

tenants   people who pay rent to use an apartment or property

testimony   a statement used for evidence or proof

tightwad   slang for miser or stingy person

traditional   handed down by custom over the years

tremor   a quick shaking movement; a vibration

trivial   not important

U

ultimate   the final; the last

unanimous   in total agreement; when everyone shares the same opinion

undoubtedly   without question; certainly

unfashionable   out of style

uproar   a condition of loud noise and confusion

usher   a doorkeeper; or one who shows people to their seats; to guide or show

V

valedictorian   the student, usually ranked highest in the class, who gives the farewell speech at graduation

verge   the extreme edge of

verified   proved the truth of

W

wads   small packs, usually of soft material
wheedled   persuaded by coaxing or flattery

Z

zeal   great enthusiasm